Unopened
LETTERS
from God

A WORKBOOK FOR INDIVIDUALS AND GROUPS

The Rev. Robert L. Haden, Jr., M Div, STM, DAPA

THE
HADEN
INSTITUTE

Cover design by Robert Lee Haden, III, HadenDesignNC.com

Haden Institute Publishing

Library of Congress Control Number: Pending

ISBN: 978-0-615-39352-0

Published in the United States of America

"The church has long known of somnia a Deo (dreams sent from God)."

C. G. JUNG

"Every local church should have the availability of a prayer group, seminars on how to pray, healing services, healing groups, and a dream group."

MORTON KELSEY

"Our culture needs to recover a sense of the sacred – that mysterious but ever present rhythm of the universe. Part of this recovery depends on taking seriously our inner life as manifested in our dreams. Dreams? Human beings have always dreamed and have been drawn to voyaging deep within to discern their inner meaning. Robert Haden provides us with a sane and grounded guide into the world of dreams. He brings to this book not only years of training others in dream work but also his own experience of discovering the wisdom imparted to us in our dreaming. What's more, dream-work is not a private trip but a way of building the human community by helping us do our own inner work and not indulge in projecting our problems and issues onto others. This then, is an immensely practical book for our fragmented times. When we take responsibility for our own inner work, the world is healed."

ALAN JONES, Dean Emeritus of Grace Cathedral, San Francisco, Founder and first Director of The Center for Christian Spirituality at General Theological Seminary, New York, NY, and author of *Soul Making, Journey Into Christ, Exploring Spiritual Direction, Reimagining Christianity, Seasons of Grace, Sacrifice and Delight, Common Prayer On Common Ground: A Vision Of Anglican Orthodoxy,* and *Passions For Pilgrimage.*

"Bob Haden offers us a valuable way of encountering dreams in the Bible and analogous themes in our own dreams. He honors dreams and texts and understands the metaphoric language of the psyche, trusting psychic process in each of us. In clear repeated steps and evocative questions, he suggests ways for us to engage Scripture and our own dreaming, and find in the spaces between them, an unfolding of ourselves and of our faith. This is a workable book, that will bring surprises where it leads."

ANN BELFORD ULANOV M.Div., Ph.D. L.H.D. Diplomate of AAPC, Christiane Brooks Johnson Professor of Psychiatry and Religion Union Theological Seminary, a psychoanalyst in private practice, and among her books, *The Unshuttered Heart: Opening to Aliveness and Deadness in the Self,* and with Barry Ulanov, *Primary Speech: A Psychology of Prayer.*

"Carl Jung has been an inspiration to religious writers and seekers for more than 100 years, and his work continues to energize and support contemporary spiritual explorers today, as this wonderful little book by Robert Haden demonstrates. Don't let the comfortable size fool you - this is a profound, and extraordinarily comprehensive work, and at the same time, it is so clearly written that it makes even the most paradoxical and complex aspects of archetypal psycho-spiritual development understandable and available to attentive readers, even if they are just beginning the great journey of self-awareness that leads simultaneously to deeper self-knowledge and more direct experience of the Divine. The exercises that readers are invited to undertake with their own dreams have all been extensively field tested and refined over the years by the people in The Haden Institute's training programs in projective *dream work and spiritual direction, and are now made available to everyone, along with wonderful insights into the deeper implications of the dreams in the Bible."*

JEREMY TAYLOR, Past President of The International Association for the Study of Dreams, Unitarian Universalist Minister and author of *The Wisdom of Dreams, Dream Work,* and *The Living Labyrinth.*

"Building a bridge with Bible stories, Unopened Letters From God provides practicing Christians an accessible crossing point into the wondrous land of dreamwork, where the guidance of the Holy Spirit still flows forth as strongly today as it did in ancient days. After a lifetime of church ministry, Robert Haden knows from experience how to lead the average person in the pews by easy-to-follow steps toward an ever deeper comprehension of the working of God in our daily and nightly lives. This book helps Christianity reclaim its legitimate birthright: the world of dreams, visions, and meaningful coincidences that has guided the people of God from earliest times, and would guide us still if we could but remember how to listen."

JOYCE ROCKWOOD HUDSON, author of *Natural Spirituality*, founder and past editor of *The Rose*, and recipient of four major book awards including Georgia Author of the Year in Fiction.

"Bob Haden brilliantly brings the lessons of the divine into our personal lives by weaving the dreams of biblical times into a working journal for our own dreams. It is a brilliantly interactive journal which takes us step by step through a wealth of proven techniques. This book is a convincing example that the divine presence can be experienced through our visions, dreams, and meditative states. It is not only a "must read" but a "must do."

BOB HOSS, Past President, the International Association for the Study of Dreams, Director, Dream Science Foundation and author of *Dream Language.*

"After having worked Bob Haden's book with my own dreams, I will never again fail to open those mysteriously instructive letters from God."

CATHY SMITH BOWERS, Poet Laureate of North Carolina and author of *The Love That Ended Yesterday In Texas, Traveling In Times of Danger, A book of Minutes,* and *The Candle I Hold Up to See You.*

"Bob Haden's new book uses time-honored stories from sacred Scripture to invite our own journey into the richness of dreams. The book is a remarkable blending of insights for dream work in a practical workbook format that carries those insights into our own work with dreams. It is an excellent primer for those newly drawn to serious dream work, but his approachable style provides new insights for even veteran dream workers."

THE RT. REV. LARRY MAZE, Episcopal Bishop of Arkansas (Ret.).

For Mary Anne, who has been my main support, partner and friend throughout the journey.

For Robert, Jimmy and Will, the three best sons anyone could ask for.

For North Carolina Poet Laureate Cathy Smith Bowers who mentored me chapter by chapter.

TABLE OF CONTENTS

INTRODUCTION

The ancient Hebrews and early Christians claimed that one of the primary ways God speaks to God's people is through dreams: not "a" way, but the "primary" way. And in his book, The 72 Names of God, Kabbalist Rabbi Yehuda Berg tells us that one of the very names of God is הלל, three Hebrew letters meaning "Dream State." Origin, the third century Christian theologian from Alexandria, Egypt, reflected this belief when he spoke of *Somnia Deo*, "Dreams sent from God." The third century Babylonian sage Rabbi Hisda put it even more succinctly: "A dream uninterpreted is like a letter (from God) unopened."

We are such stuff as dreams are made of.

SHAKESPEARE

Unfortunately, along the way, people were discouraged from taking their dreams so seriously. Jerome, the fourth century biblical scholar who authored the Vulgate Bible, translating the Greek Bible into Latin, made several mistranslations that discouraged paying attention to one's dreams. There are 10 passages in the Old Testament that use the word "anan," Latin for "witchcraft." In two of these passages, Leviticus 19:26 and Deuteronomy 18:10, Jerome used the Latin "observo somnia" (observing dreams) rather than "anan." The sentence "you shall not practice witchcraft" became "you shall not practice observing dreams." The influential sixth century Pope Gregory the Great read this translation and began to discourage people from giving too much attention to dreams. It is interesting that the eastern Christian world, which continued with the Greek Bible rather than the Vulgate Latin translation, remained dedicated to the practice of honoring dreams.

An even greater detriment to taking dreams seriously was the Enlightenment. Limiting our knowledge to things we can see, hear, taste, touch or feel eliminates not only the reality of the dream world but much of the spiritual world as well. People no longer believed dreams were "real" and therefore discounted them.

Remembering dreams is like irrigating a field, watering a garden, or planting seeds in the ground.

JOHN SANFORD

As we arrive at the end of a century of materialism a millennium of moralism, many are confessing to a thirst in their souls for a different way, for something more.

THOMAS MOORE

I, too, was a non-believer in the reality of the dream world for 40 years. Nothing anyone could have said would have changed my mind. I had to experience the reality of the dream world for myself. At the age of 40 the "God is dead" syndrome caught up with me and I began to question much of what I believed. Following the advice of a spiritual guide I went for four days of silence at the Jesuit Center for Spiritual Growth in Wernersville, PA. Prior to this life-changing experience, I had never been in one day of silence. I was soon climbing the walls and wanted desperately to flee. Nevertheless, I stayed, long enough for the inner voice to break through. Once again, I experienced the Divine Presence.

Coming off of that experience I wanted a new spirituality for myself. After getting advice from priest and Jungian analyst Morton Kelsey, I began working on my own dreams with a Jungian analyst. My ten years with her proved to be some of the most valuable experience I have ever had. I also attended the C. G. Jung Institute winter seminar in Zurich and completed a Master's program in the use of dreams in spiritual direction at the Center for Christian Spirituality at General Seminary in New York City.

I have recorded hundreds of dreams, integrating dream work with my priestly, spiritual direction and counseling duties. The riches acquired during this incubation period led to the formation of The Haden Institute.

Since my enlightenment I have made many discoveries:

> Dreams are crazy. Real crazy. They appear crazy to us because they are not literal, but rather metaphorical, like Jesus' parables. Metaphor is the primary language of the Divine. Metaphor takes us to a deeper level of awareness. So, the first thing to do with dreams is to look at them metaphorically. If your neighbor, in waking life, throws trash on your yard that is exactly what is happening. But if you dream that your neighbor throws trash on your yard,

it might be wise to see how a part of yourself is trashing (putting down) another aspect of yourself. When we look at dreams this way, insights begin to pop.

Dreams are autonomous. They are like another personality in us. They have a life of their own. Amazing.

Dreams deepen our belief in the afterlife. The aborigines believe that we come from the dream world at birth and return to the dream world after death. Dreams themselves point to a continuation beyond this life.

Is it not known to all people that the dream is the most usual way of God's revelation to humankind?

TERTULLIAN

Many conversions, inventions, healings, vocational and other life changes have come through dreams as well as dangers averted and problems solved.

Dreams are particularly meaningful to those who have "been around the block:" those in the second half of life who have experienced dead end streets, tragedies, failures, the dark night of the soul. The dream can be our guide through this maze leading us to a place where we begin to live on a deeper level.

In a dream, in a vision of the night, when deep sleep falls upon mortals, when they slumber on their beds, then God opens their ears.

JOB 33:15-16

Dreams tell it like it is. They don't sugar coat things. They alert us when we are going down the wrong road or are in danger. They also give us hope and clues as to how to get back on the right road. Even nightmares come in the service of healing and wholeness.

This book can be used by dream groups as well as by individuals. It is a workbook that can transform your life. It is only when you put yourself into the mix that the experience becomes yours. Everyone in the group will need a workbook.

A growing cloud of witnesses to the reality of the dream world are being assembled. This book is for them also:

those who already know and experience this reality but need the support, encouragement and the wisdom of the dream community.

We often hear people say, "God doesn't speak to me." Does God speak to you? The answer is a resounding "yes," to those who know the dream world. This book will lead you step by step until all of a sudden you realize God is communicating with you in a meaningful and fulfilling way. The language is an ancient language. It is a language that takes you to a deeper place where God's glory resides.

So, let's begin the exciting journey together. We are ready to leave the station. We welcome the ancient Biblical dreamers and that luminary Carl Jung who will be traveling with us. Our first stop will be in the Israeli desert between Beersheba and Haran. ⊙

O God, my God, the night has values that day has never dreamed of.

THOMAS MERTON

6

Chapter I

CLIMBING JACOB'S LADDER

Jacob left Beersheba and went towards Haran. And he came to a certain place, and stayed there that night, because the sun had set. Taking one of the stones of the place, he put it under his head and lay down in that place to sleep. And he dreamed that there was a ladder set up on the earth, and the top of it reached to heaven, and behold, the angels of God were ascending and descending on it.

— Genesis 28:10-12

One should never forget that one dreams of oneself in the first place and almost to the exclusion of all else.

C. G. JUNG

Perhaps the most familiar dream in the Bible is Jacob's dream of the angels climbing up and down the ladder from heaven to earth and earth to heaven. When we look at dreams, it is helpful to know what has been going on in the dreamer's waking life. Jacob had just lied to his father and stolen his brother Esau's birthright. His mother was in on the conspiracy. Esau was so angry he wanted to kill Jacob, but Jacob fled for his life. So, prior to this dream Jacob is roaming the desert with a broken relationship with his family and with God. Dreams have many layers, but at least one layer of this dream is that the communication between Jacob and God is beginning again.

What, then, is the metaphorical message of Jacob's dream? Notice that Jacob is not climbing up the ladder, nor is God climbing down the ladder, but the angels ("messengers" is the literal Hebrew translation) are going back and forth. Direct communication is not fully there, but it is beginning.

A woman in our Dream Leader Training Program had a Jacob's ladder dream: "I dreamed there is a wall I have to climb and I do it grabbing chains to help me. I have a wallet in my hand. People are going by me on my left. Their way seems easier, but I keep going straight ahead. It is dark and I am scared. I make it over the top, but my wallet is gone and I am naked. A man meets me and congratulates me. I am given a new robe."

The dreamer's first thought was that this dream was about her recent move to a new location and a new identity. But then she began to feel that it was also about something much deeper, her journey from egocentricity to wholeness. She had been questioning her reasons for taking this training to be a Church Dream Group Leader, especially since her life was so comfortable. She left that comfort zone, launched out into the unknown and overcame her fears. She felt called. She put on the "new robe" and it has taken her, like Jacob, to a deeper level of life and a new attitude. But, in the process, she had to let go of her worth (wallet) as it had been defined and allow herself, like Jacob, to be vulnerable (naked).

How can this biblical dream be helpful to us in trying to unlock the meaning of our nightly dreams? A woman walked into my office and said, "I hear that you know a lot about dreams. I've been having a lot of dreams about elevators, and last week I was caught for 30 minutes on an elevator between the 29th and 30th floor of the Bank of America building. What is that all about?" I said, "I don't know, but let me ask you a question. What is going up and down in your outer life?" She laughed and said, "I am a stock broker!"

How did I know to ask her that question? (I had no idea what her answer would be.) I was asking the question out of the information given by the dream. Notice, I did not ask her what was going up and down in her inner life, but in her outer life. The clue was the elevator. We don't find many elevators in houses, but rather out in the **collective**, the outer world. If it had been steps or a ladder (as in Jacob's dream) I would have asked her what was going up and down in her inner life.

Now, this kind of clue can begin the unlocking process with many of our dreams. Here are some more personal/collective clues. A **house** in a dream usually represents you, and every room in the house is an aspect of you. On the other hand, a **hotel** or **motel** represents you out in the collective. Likewise, a **car** represents your psychic energy or spiritual self going down the highway of life or, as Jung calls it, the process of individuation. On the other hand, a **bus** or a **train** represents your energy caught up in the winds of the collective.

Let me illustrate the personal and collective aspect of dreams with the following two dreams: a house dream and a hotel/motel dream.

A House Dream

My wife, Mary Anne, dreamed she was in a gray, unused kitchen. The counters had a lot of dust on them. The voice in the dream said, "Get to work." Two months later we went to St. George's College in Jerusalem to study with 20 couples from around the world. Mary Anne wanted a cup

The dream will never tell you something you already know.

ROBERT JOHNSON

of tea. She was told to find Sidabla. Sidabla took her to an old kitchen to make some tea. When she walked into the kitchen, it was like the kitchen that had been in her dream. That night at supper we met the Dean of the Cathedral. The Dean was the man who had appeared in another dream.

Such unusual occurrences happen all the time. The problem is that we are so blown away by them that we tend to say "wow" and go no further. The outer appearances of things from Mary Anne's dreams certainly caught her attention, but she did not stop there. She came to me and said, "What is the kitchen in dreams?" I said, "The only thing I know is that it is the place of creativity, transformation and change." A light bulb went off in her head. The "aha" for her was that it was time to go back to college for another degree and then "get to work." She did indeed return to college for graduate work and taught art for the next 18 years. Her studies opened up her creative side represented in the dream by the kitchen.

If, in the dream, you are in the **front of the house** (porch or yard) the dream is probably about something that is "out front" that you don't mind the public seeing. But if the dream takes place in the **back yard**, it is probably something you had rather keep from public view.

If the dream takes place in the **living room**, it probably is about something in your formal "living life." However, if it is in the **den** or **playroom**, it is probably about the informal aspect of your life. The **bathroom** is the place of elimination. In some bathroom dreams, toilets are overflowing. You are getting rid of stuff you don't need. The bathroom is also the place of cleansing. It sometimes is a sign that there is some shadow work to be done. The **basement** sometimes represents your emotional self, whereas being upstairs can represent your intellectual self. The **bedroom** is the place where you go into the unconscious (go to sleep). An **empty room** signifies that there is a part of you that is available for development. A sense that **a room is there but you can't find it** is an aspect of yourself you have not yet discovered. **Halls** are connectors.

Dreams are the oil that keeps daily life running smoothly, and the journal is a good way to get that precious oil into your life.

TRISTINE RAINER

Each one of us also has our own personal associations with all of these aspects of the house. So, it is good to surface your personal associations (i.e. the bathroom is where I got spankings as a child or the living room was where I was told to be quiet and not speak). None of the above is applicable for your particular dream, unless you have an "aha." But in trying some of these on for size you often come upon an "aha" you otherwise would not notice.

A Hotel/Motel Dream

In the course of six months there were three suicides in the parish where I was Rector. The first was a youth who took drugs, listened all the time to disturbing music, became depressed and finally took his life. The second was a teenage girl who tragically shot herself in the park because a boyfriend had left her. The third was a very good artist who felt she was not good. She pulled up into the driveway of the church and shot herself knowing the church would take care of her. The Girl Scouts found her.

That night I had a dream. I was in a hotel room where a woman was comforting me. Then I went downstairs and out the backside of the hotel, which now was a motel. I went to another room of the motel and when I opened the door, I saw a horrible sight. The walls, ceiling and floor were all dirt. A woman had just been bitten in the mouth by a snake. She ran out the door with the snake still in her mouth. Several people followed her down to the lake. The dream ends with me sitting on the patio of the motel watching the scene at the lake.

That dream was about something happening to me "out there" in the collective rather than to me personally. The clue is the presence of a hotel and motel rather than a house. If I had not considered that, I may never have known why I was in a hotel room with a sexually appealing woman or in a motel room with another woman. One of the messages was that, after the third suicide in my church, I was snake bit. I needed to take care of myself. There were others who could minister to the family & friends of their loved one who had just died in such a violent way (as indicated in the dream by the people following the woman to the lake).

The women in the dream represent my **feminine side**. The first woman ministered to me with the feminine. In this respect, the dream was already healing before I took any action. I felt this healing. The second woman was showing me that my feminine side had been hurt. I needed to let myself know that and feel the hurt so it could be healed.

Both the hotel and the motel are out in the collective. The difference between them is that a motel is more transitory. The healing which I received in the hotel would be more solid and lasting. My sitting on the sidelines was temporary. I would soon leave the motel and get in my car (psychic energy) and go on down the highway of life. That dream gave me permission to take care of myself. Otherwise I would have ploughed ahead in my masculine energy not only wearing myself out, but also being less helpful to others.

Car dreams (your personal energy) and **bus** or **train** dreams (your energy caught up in the collective) can be explored in the same fashion. A train may signify that you are "on track" or that the collective energy you are caught up in has to stay on track and travel a designated track. ⊙

Dreams voice the unvarnished truth of emotions and intuitions and set a standard of personal honesty for who you really are.

TRISTINE RAINER

Unlock One of Your Dreams

This one short Biblical dream has opened up so much about the dream world. So, let's have a breather and apply what we have learned so far.

- Pick one of your dreams that have steps or ladders or elevators or houses or motels or hotels or cars or busses or trains.
- Write the dream here in the first person present tense, remembering every detail you can (In my dream I am climbing a ladder...).
- Underline any of the aforementioned objects in your dream.
- With each object write about it in the metaphorical way I talked about the dreams above.

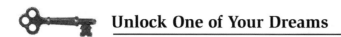

Unlock One of Your Dreams

 **Unlock One of Your Dreams**

- Now, recall what has been going on in your life recently. Can you make any connections? Where are your "ahas?" The dreamer's "aha" reveals the interpretation of the dream.

 **Unlock One of Your Dreams**

• What insights have come? Write them down.

🗝 Unlock One of Your Dreams

It is important to record your dreams in the next few days because what you missed will show up in future dreams. The dream maker keeps sending dreams until we get the message. If you got it, the dream maker will not send another dream about that particular issue. Dreams tell us only what we don't know. We are not through with this dream. We have just begun.

- In the following chapters you will be learning more about dreams. As you do, you will be revisiting this dream with your new knowledge. Write it down here.

 **Unlock One of Your Dreams**

Chapter II

WRESTLING WITH AN INNER ADVERSARY

And Jacob was left alone; and a man wrestled with him until the breaking of the day. When the man saw that he did not prevail against Jacob, he touched the hollow of his thigh; and Jacob's thigh was put out of joint as he wrestled with him. Then he said, 'let me go for the day is breaking.' But Jacob said, 'I will not let you go until you bless me.' And he said to him, 'what is your name?' And he said, 'Jacob.' Then he said, 'Your name shall no longer be called Jacob, but Israel, for you have striven with God and with men and have prevailed.'

— Genesis 32:24-28

This dream takes place some 20 years after Jacob's ladder dream. He is still on the run from his brother, Esau. He now has two wives, Leah and Rachael. After working seven years for his first bride, Rachael, he discovers, when she takes her veil off, it is not Rachael, but Leah. So, he works seven more years for Rachael. Isn't it interesting that the man who tricked his father and brother has now been tricked himself? Now, on the day of the dream, Leah and Rachael's father, Laban, comes with his men to take back Leah, Rachael, the children, and his flock. Jacob pleads and makes an agreement with Laban. However, he gets word that his brother Esau is arriving the next day with 400 men. He knows Esau will kill him. He needs a stronger self to face the next day. It is that night, after battling with his father-in-law during the day and knowing that his brother will arrive on the morrow, that he lies down and has this dream.

One does not become enlightened by imagining figures of light, but by making the darkness conscious. The latter procedure, however, is disagreeable and therefore not popular.

C. G. JUNG

Do you ever wake up from sleep feeling like you have been wrestling all night in your dreams? You feel tired and exhausted and sometimes wake up sweating with tired muscles and bones. This is how Jacob felt. He had been wrestling with something powerful.

The shadow is the dumping ground for all those characteristics of our personality that we disown.

ROBERT JOHNSON

It takes a strong ego to stand up to such powers in your dream and wrestle with them in an assertive way. A strong ego is very important. Carl Jung asserts that the first half of life is for identity and the second half of life is for meaning. The stronger our ego the deeper we can go in the second half of life. It takes a strong ego to face into the deeper issues of life and especially, as Jacob did, to stand our own ground with the divine. So, building up your own ego and helping your children to build up their ego-strength is vital and necessary.

Notice that Jacob did not have this dream earlier. He had to get strong first. The angels climbing up and down the ladder is a much softer, calmer dream than wrestling until the break of day and waking up with a wounded body. Jacob wasn't ready earlier.

Many dreams don't come until we are ready for them. Jeremy Taylor tells of a seminary student who was in a dream group for two years before he could remember a dream. He was so embarrassed that he decided to leave the dream group, but his fellow seminarians convinced him to stay. It was then that he had a dream suggesting that he would be much happier as a banker rather than a minister. So, his fellow seminarians walked him across the street and he enrolled in the business school of the university. He was not ready to receive this dream earlier. His ego was not strong enough to withstand the strong will of his parents who wanted him to be a minister. He needed the two years with these seminarians to build up a strength sturdy enough to stand up to his parents' powerful influence. The seminarians walking him across the street was a power strong enough for him to go on his own individuation journey, not his parents' journey. So, many dreams don't come until we are ready for them and building up our ego strength is most important.

The shadow personality can also be thought of as the unlived life.

JOHN SANFORD

As noted before, every person in the dream is an aspect of the dreamer himself. In this dream Jacob is wrestling with his inner adversary. He does not run from this adversary, but rather faces him and looks him square in the eye, demanding things of him and not letting him go. It is an all-night wrestle. He wakes sweating and wounded, but, as we shall see, a new man.

The shadow is at work attempting to recreate early childhood relationships with a secret mission … to heal old wounds and feel loved.

CONNIE ZWEIG

A Nightmare

Frightening figures appear in our dreams also. Our call is not to run from them, but to face them and probe them for the messages they have for us. These messages come many times in the form of nightmares. My favorite nightmare is the one told by the great dream worker, Jeremy Taylor.

The nightmare begins with a dragon chasing the dreamer, blowing fire and smoke out of its nose scorching the earth. The dreamer is running, but cannot get away. In working with this nightmare the dreamer was encouraged to get back into the dream (in the dreamer's imagination) and to face the dragon and ask, "Who are you?" The dreamer did this and the dragon answered, "I am your smoking habit."

In further conversation, the dreamer began to call him "Puff, the magic dragon" and realized that every time he was lonely he would take a "puff." Now, if his wife, doctor or priest had told him to quit smoking, he probably would have gotten defensive. But when his dream told him, he began working on both his smoking habit and his loneliness problem. One of the wonderful things about dreams is that when we hear their message, we tend not to get defensive.

So, one of the things this biblical dream teaches us is that we need to face some of the characters in our dreams rather than run from them. The payoff can be rich. This is what Jesus had to do when he went into the wilderness after his baptism and before he started his mission. He had to die to miracle ("change these stones into bread"), to magic ("jump off the temple and let your angels catch you"), and to power ("give you the whole world if you will follow me").

Because Jacob has dealt with his inner adversary, the next day he approaches his brother Esau with a different attitude. He is conciliatory. He "bows to the ground seven times" as Esau approaches with his 400 men. This changed attitude makes all the difference. Esau responds favorably embracing and kissing him. To seal the event, God changes Jacob's name from Jacob ("over-reacher") to Israel ("one who wrestles with God"). It is interesting that the Jews are not referred to as Abrahamites or Isaacites or Jacobites, but rather Israelites. Amazing what transformations can occur if we pay attention to our dreams, our letters from God. ☉

The night, O My Lord, is a time of freedom. You have seen the morning and the night, and the night was better. In the night all things began, and in the night the end of all things has come before me.

THOMAS MERTON

 **Unlock One of Your Dreams**

Unlock One of Your Dreams

• Get back into the dream in your imagination and instead of running or avoiding, face the person or animal and ask: "who are you?" and/or "What are you doing in my dream?" and see what answer your imagination gives. You can do this with paper and pencil or with two chairs with you in one chair and the person or animal in the other chair. As you continue the conversation, change chairs to become the other. Let your imagination freely flow until there is an "aha." This is called amplification or carrying the dream forward. Write down the conversation.

Unlock One of Your Dreams

 **Unlock One of Your Dreams**

• What insights have come? Write them down.

Unlock One of Your Dreams

It is important to record your dreams in the next few days because what you missed will show up in future dreams. The dream maker keeps sending dreams until we get the message. If you got it, the dream maker will not send another dream about that particular issue. Dreams tell us only what we don't know. We are not through with this dream. We have just begun.

- Does anything you have learned in this chapter give you additional insights into the dreams you worked in the previous chapters? Go back and write it down.
- In the following chapters you will be learning more about dreams. As you do, you will be revisiting this dream with your new knowledge. Write it down here.

Chapter III

JOSEPH'S JOURNEY THROUGH HELL TO WHOLENESS

*Now Joseph had a dream, and when he told it to his brothers
they only hated him the more. He said to them, 'Hear this dream
which I have dreamed: behold, we were binding sheaves in the
field, and lo, my sheaf arose and stood upright; and behold your
sheaves gathered round it, and bowed down to my sheaf.'*

— Genesis 37:5-7

Joseph is one of the foremost biblical interpreters of dreams. But there is trouble in his family, as we have already experienced with his parents, grandparents and great-grandparents and all the in-laws. We will see how this family dysfunction plays into his dreams.

A human being has so many skins inside, covering the depths of the heart. We know so many things, but we don't know ourselves! Go into your own ground and learn to know yourself there.

MEISTER ECKHART

But let's first catch up with the story. We last left Joseph's father, Jacob, at Peniel where, in a dream, he wrestles with an inner adversary. Afterwards, his name is changed from Jacob to Israel because he has "struggled with God and man and [has] overcome." Following this dream he faces his brother, Esau, and his 400 soldiers. He bows to the ground seven times, but Esau, his outer adversary, runs to meet him. They kiss and weep. Then there is a grand reunion of all the wives, concubines, children and relatives who have always known about each other, but never met. Then the two brothers, their livestock and families go, happily, their separate ways.

Jacob later returns to Bethel (where he had his first dream), settles there and builds an altar because that is where God first revealed himself to him. Later they leave Bethel for Ephrath (that is Bethlehem). On the way Rachel dies as she is giving birth to Benjamin. Jacob (now Israel) has twelve sons, who later become the beginning of the twelve tribes of Israel. The youngest of the twelve is Joseph.

Jacob "loves Joseph more than his other children" because Joseph is born in Jacob's old age. He gives him a special "coat of many colors" (literally, in the Hebrew, a special coat with long sleeves). What a set-up for trouble in the family! This special attention causes Joseph to be arrogant and his brothers to hate him. We have seen this dynamic in many a family.

Joseph does become one of the foremost biblical interpreters of dreams; but, like Native Americans and ancient shamans, he has to go through his own hell in order to have the depth, maturity, wisdom, authenticity and authority needed for such a high calling.

What is true of Joseph and the shamans is true for us if we are to follow our journey to wholeness or, as Carl Jung calls it, our path of individuation. This journey begins with our birth and the response to our environment. We, like Joseph, respond to the fate of our particular life situation with adaptations and inflations. Many people get stuck right here and live the rest of their life with their particular adaptations and inflations. They play it safe and refuse to become conscious. Carl Jung defines sin as "purposely refusing to become conscious."

If we are to progress any further in life, we must go through the dark night of the soul, which cleanses us like a purifying fire. Some, indeed, think they are playing it safe, only to have their shadows erupt, thrusting them into the dark night. Mid-life crises are a vivid picture of this dynamic. Most of us, like Jonah in the biblical story of "Jonah and the whale," have to be pushed into the ocean for the "deep sea journey" (as the dark night is sometimes called).

So it is with Joseph. He, very naively, strikes out on this journey as an arrogant 17 year old. His father has just given him the coat of many colors. His brothers hate him. And when he tells the dream about his brothers' sheaves bowing down to his sheaf, they get livid and want to kill him. Instead they put him in a deep hole to leave him to die. A caravan going to Egypt finds him and takes him to Egypt where he is imprisoned twice. Joseph, later, becomes Secretary of State in Egypt and his brothers have to come to him for grain because there has been a seven-year famine in the land. So, the original dream proves true. The brothers do, indeed, have to bow down to him.

When the ego follows the signals given in dreams, it is helping the Self attain realization in time and space.

MARIE-LOUISE VON FRANZ

In the middle of the journey of our life I came to myself in a dark wood where the straight way was lost.

DANTE ALIGHIERI

The problem is that Joseph has told this dream with an inflated, arrogant, egocentric attitude. He is unaware how inflated he is and how dangerous an arrogant attitude can be. If we are conscious of our inflation, we can bring ourselves down bit by bit. But if we are not conscious of the inflation, we will most likely drop into a depression following the high feeling. The depression, usually, responds in like kind to the length and depth of the inflation.

Dreams tell us when we are inflated. I once had a dream that I was on a rickety tower 1000 feet above the coast of Costa Rica, thrilled with the fantastic view. Then I suddenly realized I could fall if I remained up there much longer. Later, I got back into the dream—in my imagination--and was able to bring myself down bit by bit. This use of active imagination helped me come down from my waking-life inflation rather than sink into depression for the next several days.

One of the helpful things that dreams do every night is to give us a snapshot of our life at the present moment, especially the dynamics, of which we are not aware. When we don't discover the message of the dream by doing our inner work, outer things begin to happen.

When Jonah wouldn't pay attention to the inner message from God, "a storm rose up around him." My guess is that when TV-evangelists Jimmy Swaggart and Jim Baker wouldn't listen to their inner messages, outer storms rose up around them (jail for one and public humiliation for the other). The same might be said of Martha Stewart. And when I, myself, wouldn't listen to the multitude of inner messages to leave parish ministry and start The Haden Institute, a storm rose up in the parish, causing me, like Jonah, to jump. Joseph's outer storm was his brothers leaving him in a pit to die and then imprisonment in Egypt.

Joseph's imprisonment, Baker and Stewart's jail terms, Swaggart's front-page prostitution story, and my parish storm catapulted us into the dark night of the soul. We did not know it, but these storms were gifts, necessary steps toward our becoming servant leaders. The purpose of dark nights is to purify us to the extent that egocentric inflation is kept to a level that does not interfere with servant living and leading. Joseph, through listening to his dreams and following his path of individuation, moves from egocentricity to wholeness, to that person God is calling him to be.

Maltese Cross Inflation Dream

When I was just beginning my own study of dreams, I had a dream of a picture on the front page of a church newsletter. The picture was of a priest friend kneeling down at a church kneeler holding a Maltese Cross saying his prayers. My immediate response upon awaking was to cringe. I said out loud, "John, why do you want to say your private prayers in front of the whole congregation!"

We learned earlier that everyone in most of our dreams is an aspect of us. So, who is John in the dream? That's right— John is Bob. Bob is "saying his private prayers in front of the whole congregation." And what did we learn about the importance of metaphor. What, metaphorically, does this image represent in Bob's life? I was so inflated with my new knowledge of dreams that I was telling everybody my just-fresh-from-the-unconscious dreams. My analyst pointed out that dreams are like our private prayer life. They are not to be shared around with everybody, at least until they get some age and maturity and inflation-decontamination. So, the dream is about my inflation and showing off, not John's.

Knowing that every detail in the dream is important, my analyst asked, "What is the Maltese Cross to you?" I said, "It has always been appealing to me, but I have no idea what it means." She said, "If it were me, I would want to find out." When I woke up at 4am the next morning I said, "Why wait?" I got out my encyclopedias and began by looking up Maltese Cross. It was the cross of the Hospitalers in Jerusalem. Their patron Saint was John. Looking up John led me to John of the Cross. The encyclopedic-5am-words read: "at about the age of 40, John of the Cross's

I went down

Into the cavern

All the way down

To the bottom of the sea.

I went down lower

Than Jonas and the whale

No one ever got so far down

As me.

No matter how

They try to harm me now

No matter where

They lay me in the grave

No matter what injustices

they do

I've seen the root

Of all that believe.

But when they thought

I was gone forever

That I was all the way

In hell

I got right back into my body

And came back out

And rang my bell..

THOMAS MERTON

I came back from the most holy waves, born Again, even as new trees renewed with new Foliage, pure and ready to mount to the Stars.

DANTE ALIGHIERI

spiritual director (Teresa of Avila) said to him, 'John, this is your personal private prayer life and you are talking about it too much in public.' "

I was 40 and had not heard of John of the Cross or Teresa of Avila, the great Spanish mystics of the Carmelite tradition. Twenty years later I realized I had been Rector of St. John's Church on Carmel Road and that now The Haden Institute has expanded to, and joined with, the Carmelite Spiritual Centre in Canada where we teach the spirituality of Teresa of Avila, John of The Cross and all the great mystics.

Dreams have many levels. My dream, like Joseph's, had both an inflation and prophetic level. In both cases the inflation had to be dealt with before the prophetic could come to fruition. ○

 **Unlock One of Your Dreams**

• Pick a dream (as close to the present time as possible) that suggests a feeling of inflation. Write it down in the first person present tense.

 **Unlock One of Your Dreams**

Unlock One of Your Dreams

- Now, ask yourself, where in my waking life (at the time of the dream) did I feel inflated? Write it down. What was the inflation about? Do you feel inflated now? What is the inflation about now? Where am I thinking of myself more highly than I ought? Real humility, in the biblical understanding, is not being a doormat allowing people to run over you, but rather seeing yourself, as you are, no more, no less.

 **Unlock One of Your Dreams**

Unlock One of Your Dreams

- Is there anything we learned about dreams in the first two chapters that is also helpful with this dream?
- Does this dream have houses or hotels or cars or buses or anything that indicates whether this dream is about your private world or you out in the collective?
- Is there anything you are running from in this dream? Face it (in your imagination) and ask, "Who are you and what are you doing in my dream?"

 **Unlock One of Your Dreams**

• What insights have come? Write them down.

Unlock One of Your Dreams

It is important to record your dreams in the next few days because what you missed will show up in future dreams. The dream maker keeps sending dreams until we get the message. If you got it, the dream maker will not send another dream about that particular issue. Dreams tell us only what we don't know. We are not through with this dream. We have just begun.

- Does anything you have learned in this chapter give you additional insights into the dreams you worked in the previous chapters? Go back and write it down.
- In the following chapters you will be learning more about dreams. As you do, you will be revisiting this dream with your new knowledge. Write it down here.

Chapter IV

PHARAOH'S REPETITIVE DREAMS

Then Pharaoh said to Joseph, "In my dream I was standing on the brink of the Nile, when out of the river came up seven cows, fat and sleek, and they grazed among the reeds. After them seven other cows came up – scrawny and very ugly and lean. I had never seen such ugly cows in all the land of Egypt. The lean, ugly cows ate up the seven fat cows that came up first. But even after they ate them, no one could tell that they had done so; they looked just as ugly as before. Then I woke up."

— Genesis 41:17-21

Since we last left Joseph, he has been in prison twice and received the fury of Pharaoh's wife for refusing her sexual advances. (I love that story. It begins "Joseph was well built and handsome…." Read it beginning with the 39th chapter of Genesis.) While in prison the second time, he interpreted the dreams of two prisoners. The Pharaoh was so impressed he asked Joseph to interpret two dreams that were haunting him.

Joseph's answer to this request is interesting. He tells the Pharaoh, "I cannot do it, but God will give Pharaoh the answer he desires." Joseph is acknowledging that God is the interpreter, as well as the giver, of the dream. That is, it is God's Spirit working in us that interprets the dream rather than our analyst, counselor, priest, or shaman (all of whom can be helpful and sometimes crucial).

Pharaoh's Second Dream

I saw seven heads of grain, full and good, growing on a single stalk. After them, seven other heads sprouted – withered and thin and scorched by the east wind. The thin heads of grain swallowed up the good heads. I told these to the magicians, but none of them could explain it to me.

This was Pharaoh's second dream. So, if the dream interpreter doesn't get it, the dream keeps coming back (in a little different form) in hopes the shaman and/or dreamer will get it this time. This is why dreams following counseling or spiritual direction or dream group sessions are so valuable. They tell us what we missed. The dream is one of my greatest guides in spiritual direction and counseling.

Joseph's interpretation (the Spirit working through Joseph) is that there will be seven years of plenty and seven years of famine because of a drought in the land. His wise advice is to store up some of the wheat in barns for seven years so Egypt will have wheat when the drought comes. The Pharaoh is so pleased with this dream (which must have felt

like an "aha" to him) that he made Joseph Secretary of State
to set the plan in motion.

Then Joseph's 17-year-old-inflation/prophetic dream comes
to fruition. His brothers do, indeed, come to him ("bow
down to him") for food during the famine. As a result,
Joseph and his brothers become reconciled. "What you
intended for harm, God meant for good." These were
Joseph's healing words to his brothers. "What you intended
for harm, God meant for good." God works in mysterious
ways God's wonders to perform. And God keeps sending us
the message until we get it.

In working with hundreds of dreams of others I have found
Joseph's advice to be true. I can be very helpful to others
circumambulating (walking around) their dreams, especially
with the knowledge I now have. But it has been my
experience that the Spirit leads us to the interpretation of
the dream. For that reason, when I am at my best, I begin
working with a dream not knowing where I am going. I
allow the dream to lead in the questions I ask.

Pharaoh's second dream is similar to the first one. It is a
good example of a repetitive dream. Joseph knew this was
important because he himself had had a repetitive dream.
Repetitive dreams are important ones to pay attention to.
We have repetitive dreams because we have not gotten the
message yet. So, the dream maker sends another picture
to us. Similar dreams keep coming until we get it. Abused
and troubled children have similar dreams until they are out
of the abusive or troubled situation or become conscious of
it and acknowledge it.

A Teenager's Repetitive Dream

A Youth Minister brought a 17-year-old girl to me. Every
night at the youth retreat, she had been in a fetal position
having a nightmare. Her screaming and yelling frightened
the other kids. I asked Jennifer to tell me the nightmare.
She said, "In the nightmare I am holding a gigantic boulder
on my shoulders. I can no longer hold it and there is a

person lying at my feet that I fear the boulder will crush." After acknowledging what a horrible nightmare that was, I asked her, "Who is lying on the ground?"

"It looks a little bit like my sister and a little bit like me," she said.

"Tell me about your sister," I said.

"My sister has been retarded since birth and I am her primary caretaker. My parents do not care for her much at all."

At this juncture, my more normal non-directive self got very directive. I told her, "Go home and tell your parents that they have to become the primary caretakers now. If you don't, the dream is telling us that the boulder is not only going to fall on your sister, but on you as well."

When Jennifer came into my office, I had no idea where I was going with this dream or what questions I was going to ask. But as I heard the dream, leading questions began to appear. Even at this point, I had no idea where this was headed. When we trust the dream and the process, the Spirit has a better environment in which to work. I don't deny that my knowledge of dreams was very helpful in knowing what to inquire of the dream. But one of the cardinal rules of dream work is to allow yourself to be led by the dream. ◎

 ## Unlock One of Your Dreams

• Pick a repetitive dream. Write it down in the first person present tense.

Unlock One of Your Dreams

 **Unlock One of Your Dreams**

- Now, ask yourself, when did I first have this dream? What was going on in my life at the time? How has it continued? When did it stop? Did the dreams stop when the life issue was solved or acknowledged or acted on?
- If you unlock this repetitive dream, you will unlock something the dream maker has been trying to communicate to you for some time.

Unlock One of Your Dreams

Unlock One of Your Dreams

- Do any of the earlier learnings apply to this dream? Use anything you have learned so far to try to unlock this dream.
- Is there anything to be faced in this dream?
- Is there anything that distinguishes whether it is about your personal or collective energies?
- Does the dream indicate any inflation?

 **Unlock One of Your Dreams**

• What insights have come? Write them down.

Unlock One of Your Dreams

It is important to record your dreams in the next few days because what you missed will show up in future dreams. The dream maker keeps sending dreams until we get the message. If you got it, the dream maker will not send another dream about that particular issue. Dreams tell us only what we don't know. We are not through with this dream. We have just begun.

- Does anything you have learned in this chapter give you additional insights into the dreams you worked in the previous chapters? Go back and write it down.
- In the following chapters you will be learning more about dreams. As you do, you will be revisiting this dream with your new knowledge. Write it down here.

 **Unlock One of Your Dreams**

Chapter V

MIRIAM'S JEALOUSY

Miriam and Aaron began to talk against Moses, because of his Cushite wife, for he had married a Cushite. 'Has the Lord spoken only through Moses?' they asked. 'Hasn't he also spoken through us?' And The Lord heard this. At once the Lord said to Moses, Aaron and Miriam, 'come out to the Tent of Meeting, all three of you.' So the three of them came out. Then the Lord came down in a pillar of cloud; he stood at the entrance to the tent and summoned Miriam and Aaron. When both of them stepped forward, he said, 'Listen to my words:

> *When a prophet of the Lord is among you,*
> > *I reveal myself in visions,*
> > *I speak to him in dreams.*
> *But this is not true of my servant Moses,*
> > *He is faithful in all my house.*
> *With him I speak face to face,*
> > *Clearly and not in riddles;*
> > *He sees the form of the Lord.*
> *Why then were you not afraid*
> > *To speak against my servant Moses?'*

— Numbers 12:1-8

Miriam is a prophetess of the Lord and the sister of Moses and Aaron. God speaks to her through dreams and she prophesies. But she gets jealous because Yahweh seems to favor her brother Moses. Yahweh cuts through this jealousy the moment he hears it. Yahweh calls Miriam and Aaron to come stand in front of the Tent of Meeting (the Holy of Holies, the place where God is especially present, the church where the people of God gather) to give them a piece of his mind.

Yahweh tells them that he does, indeed, speak with them through visions and dreams as he does with many of his prophets and prophetesses, but Moses is in a different sphere now – Yahweh speaks mystically to Moses face to face, without metaphor. Moses, a deeply spiritual person, goes up on the mountain and floats into the numinous world. Yahweh's distinction does not in any way demean Miriam and Aaron, but puts them in their place, in the good sense of the word. The jealousy vanishes.

Jealousy is, indeed, a complex emotion. Thomas Moore, Jesuit author of *Care of the Soul*, suggests that when jealousy crops up in us, we should try not to repress it, but rather allow it to be there long enough to know what the deeper soul issue is. Miriam thinks her jealousy is about Moses marrying a Cushite wife. In a sense it is. But under that surface jealousy is a deeper felt fear that the Lord loves her brother Moses more than her. She needs to be hit square in the face with this reality and then have time to think about it. So, Yahweh strikes her with leprosy, but through Aaron's protest and Moses' pleading, Miriam is healed after spending seven days separated from the community. The whole community waits also. They do not move on until Miriam's seven days of healing are over.

So much wisdom lies in this story. The thing that will stop a **negative animus** (whining, etc.) is a strong **positive animus** (Yahweh calling them out of the Tent of Meeting and saying, "Listen to me!"). A positive animus can stop a negative animus dead in its tracks. We think we know what our jealousy (depression, frustration, etc.) is about, but usually there is something deeper underneath. When a new understanding (revelation) comes, we need to sit with it for a while (go apart from the community for seven days). The community has to wait while one of its members heals. Then it can healthily move forward unified.

I came home one day feeling a deep sense of jealousy. My wife Mary Anne was now going to put on her blue jeans and go back to college for additional study. I just knew she was going to fly off with one of the professors. When I told my wife, she laughed at me. I tried to repress the jealousy, but it would not repress.

So, I took Thomas Moore's advice and sat down with it for a while. As I was sitting there probing "what is the deeper soul issue here," a deep insight accompanied by an "aha" feeling arose. It suddenly occurred to me that I had been "out in the world" and Mary Anne had been "at home." Now she was also going to be "out in the world." There was going to be a change in the power structure in our relationship. Our relationship was moving to one of equal power.

I like that relationship much better, but at the time it was a major shift and my psyche had to adjust. The fear of losing Mary Anne served the purpose of stopping me dead in my tracks. The "sitting down" time enabled my deeper wisdom to arise.

Miriam's story is my story. Perhaps if I had been more attentive to my own dreams at the time, it would not have taken so much "sitting." ✲

 **Unlock One of Your Dreams**

- Pick a dream that has a heavy feeling of jealousy (or frustration, or depression or hate, etc.). Write it down in the first person present tense.

Unlock One of Your Dreams

Unlock One of Your Dreams

• Try not to repress the feeling, but bring it back in full force by asking, "where in my waking life do I find this feeling that was in my dream?" Take enough time to be with this feeling so you can discover what the deeper soul issue is.

 **Unlock One of Your Dreams**

Unlock One of Your Dreams

- Use anything you have learned so far to try to unlock this dream
- Do any of the earlier learnings apply to this dream?
- Is there anything to be faced in this dream?
- Is there anything that distinguishes whether it is about your personal or collective energies?
- Does the dream indicate any inflation?
- Is there anything you are running from or avoiding in this dream?

 **Unlock One of Your Dreams**

• What insights have come? Write them down.

Unlock One of Your Dreams

It is important to record your dreams in the next few days because what you missed will show up in future dreams. The dream maker keeps sending dreams until we get the message. If you got it, the dream maker will not send another dream about that particular issue. Dreams tell us only what we don't know. We are not through with this dream. We have just begun.

- Does anything you have learned in this chapter give you additional insights into the dreams you worked in the previous chapters? Go back and write it down.
- In the following chapters you will be learning more about dreams. As you do, you will be revisiting this dream with your new knowledge. Write it down here.

 **Unlock One of Your Dreams**

Chapter VI

VOICES IN THE NIGHT

*One night Eli, whose eyes were becoming so weak that he could
barely see, was lying down in his usual place. The lamp of God
was not yet out, and Samuel was lying down in the temple of the
Lord, where the ark of God was. Then the Lord called Samuel.
Samuel answered, 'Here I am.' And he ran to Eli and said, 'Here
I am; you called me.' But Eli said, 'I did not call; go back and
lie down.' So he went and lay down. Again the Lord called,
'Samuel!' And Samuel got up and went to Eli and said, 'Here
I am; you called me.' 'My son,' Eli said, 'I did not call; go back
and lie down.' Now Samuel did not yet know the Lord; the word
of the Lord had not yet been revealed to him. The Lord called
Samuel a third time, and Samuel got up and went to Eli and
said, 'Here I am; you called me.' Eli realized the Lord was calling
Samuel and he told him to say, 'Speak Lord, for your servant
is listening.' The Lord came and stood there calling as at other
times, 'Samuel! Samuel!' Then Samuel said, 'Speak Lord, for
your servant is listening.'*

— I Samuel 3:2-10

It is necessary that we find the silence of God not only in ourselves but also in one another.

THOMAS MERTON

Samuel is having an **incubation dream**. Incubation dreams are ones produced in holy places. Samuel, whose mother Hannah had dedicated him to the temple, has a dream incubated in the temple at Shiloh. The dream comes to him in the form of voices in the night. Voices in dreams normally indicate a message straight from God, the **Self**, the Divine within us. It sometimes takes a while for us to believe it or take in such a phenomenon. Samuel hears the voice three times before he figures out who is speaking. And that is only with the help of Eli, who is steeped in the spiritual world. Eli has experienced such voices in the night, but Samuel is new to God's voice and needs a spiritual director for interpretation.

We visited such a holy place on a Haden Institute pilgrimage to Greece. The holy place was at Epidaurus, the most famous shrine of Aesculapius. Aesculapius was a renowned healer and the forerunner of Western medicine. Dreams were purposely incubated at this 370 BC Aesculapian temple as part of the healing process. Priests would offer some evening prayers or hymns, as well as purification rites, sacrifices and prayers, in the temple during the "hour of sacred lamps." The people seeking healing would pray to Aesculapius to give them a dream. Healers would use these dreams to help in the diagnostic process.

Many people experience the same thing when they go on retreat to a monastery or other holy place. The prayers, candles, incense, stained glass, statues, ritual, gardens, quiet, and holy people (present and past) whose spirits fill the atmosphere are all conducive to incubating dreams.

A participant coming to a Haden Institute Summer Dream Conference at Kanuga Conference Center had such an experience. She was tired and decided to skip the evening session. That night in her dream she found herself at the evening session. The speaker looked directly at her. "Read Romans 2:29," he said. She, of course, got out her Bible and read Romans 2:29 and surrounding verses. The passage was about circumcision. She was confused. She brought the dream to her conference dream group. As the group

circumambulated (walked around) her dream, she made a
connection. She had just come from Africa taking pictures
of impoverished children for a photography book. The last
place she visited she was disturbed to learn about young
girls being circumcised. She could not help any of the
wives, but by taking a risk, she was able to work through
the wives to protect some of their daughters from unwanted
circumcision. Her compassion enabled her to take the
risk. The dream, among other things, was confirming the
holiness of her concern and her identifying with suffering
the world over. Many people have shared with me dreams
that have been incubated at Kanuga, which, before it was
a Christian holy place, was a Native American holy place.
Well-known author and speaker, Madeleine L'Engle, claims
Kanuga is one of the "thin places" on this earth where the
winds of the Spirit blow stronger.

*Wisdom comes to us
in dreams.*
    SMOHALLA, NEZ PERCE INDIAN

Samuel's dream is not only an example of incubating
dreams, but also of the fact that dreams sometimes give us
unpleasant messages as well as pleasant ones. And we, like
Samuel, don't want to bring that unpleasantness to the light
of day.

Now, here comes the most interesting part of the dream.
Samuel did as Eli suggested and responded by saying,
"Speak, for your servant is listening." Surprise! God didn't
say, "What a nice boy you are. Keep at it and you will
grow up to be a good priest like Eli." But rather he said, "I
am about to do something in Israel that will make the ears
of everyone who hears it tingle." And he proceeds to tell
Samuel that he wants him to deliver the bad news.

The bad news is that God is going to punish Eli because
his sons have been contestable and Eli has not spoken
against them. Samuel, like most of us, does not want to
deliver this bad news. He is afraid to tell Eli everything.
And the wise Eli senses he isn't telling the whole story. He
says "Do not hide it from me," even if it is bad news. So,
Samuel tells him everything. Eli responds, "He is the Lord;
let him do what is good in his eyes." His response is not a
defensive one. Here is another example that when we hear

confronting news from dreams, unlike from other people, we tend not to get defensive.

Carl Jung had such a dream, actually a vision. The vision was so disgusting to him that he would not allow it to surface. This is how Jung tells the experience:

> *One fine summer day that same year I came out of school at noon and went to the cathedral square. The sky was gloriously blue, the day one of radiant sunshine. The roof of the cathedral was glittering, the sun sparkling from the new, brightly glazed tiles. I was overwhelmed by the beauty of the sight, and thought: 'The world is beautiful and the church is beautiful, and God made all this and sits far away in the blue sky on a golden throne and...' Here came a great hole in my thoughts, and a choking sensation. I felt numbed: and knew only: 'Don't go on thinking now! Something terrible is coming, something I don't want to think, something I dare not even approach. I would be committing the most frightful of all sins, the sin against the Holy Ghost, which cannot be forgiven.*

The most religious places in the world have the darkest shadow.

C. G. JUNG

This "something inside of him" was so horrible to him that every time it came to his mind, he would repress it. Three days later in the middle of the night he could hold it back no longer.

> *I gathered all my courage, as though I was about to leap forthwith into hell-fire, and let the thought come. I saw before me the cathedral, the blue sky. God sits on his golden throne, high above the world – and from under the golden throne an enormous turd falls upon the sparkling new roof, shatters it, and breaks the walls of the cathedral asunder.*

When he finally dealt with this vision he realized that, at least on one level, the dream had to do with the church in his day. He felt that his father, a Swiss Protestant Minister, did not understand God's Grace. He feared that the church was losing the experience of the Divine. And if it lost the experience of the Divine, the church would go down the drain. And if the church went down the drain, Western civilization would go down the drain. This fear led Jung into his fallow, hermit stage, a period of about six years during which he experienced the Divine on a deeper level.

✺

As from a dream one may
  awake to find,
Its passion yet imprinted on
  the heart,
Although all else is cancelled
  from the mind,

So of my vision now but
  little part,
Remains, yet in my inmost
  soul I know,
The sweet instilling which it
  did impart.

DANTE ALIGHIERI

 ## Unlock One of Your Dreams

- Have you had an incubated dream, a dream that came to you in a holy place or near holy surroundings? Write it down in the first person present tense.

 **Unlock One of Your Dreams**

 **Unlock One of Your Dreams**

• Now, ask yourself, "What was the message for my life?"

 **Unlock One of Your Dreams**

• Write down a dream that had an unpleasant message in it.

Unlock One of Your Dreams

 **Unlock One of Your Dreams**

- What was the unpleasant message and why did you not want to tell it?
- Did you ever tell it, accept it yourself, or is it still inside you?
- What do you fear if you told it or dealt with it yourself?

Unlock One of Your Dreams

- Use anything you have learned so far to try to unlock this dream.
- Do any of the earlier learnings apply to this dream?
- Are the energies in the dream personal or collective?
- Is there any person or thing in the dream you need to confront and dialogue with to get more insight?

 **Unlock One of Your Dreams**

• What insights have come? Write them down.

Unlock One of Your Dreams

It is important to record your dreams in the next few days because what you missed will show up in future dreams. The dream maker keeps sending dreams until we get the message. If you got it, the dream maker will not send another dream about that particular issue. Dreams tell us only what we don't know. We are not through with this dream. We have just begun.

- Does anything you have learned in this chapter give you additional insights into the dreams you worked in the previous chapters? Go back and write it down.
- In the following chapters you will be learning more about dreams. As you do, you will be revisiting this dream with your new knowledge. Write it down here.

 **Unlock One of Your Dreams**

Chapter VII

EZEKIEL'S VISION OF THE CHARIOT

I looked, and I saw a windstorm coming out of the north – an immense cloud with flashing lightning and surrounded by brilliant light. The center of the fire looked like glowing metal, and in the fire was what looked like four living creatures. In appearance their form was that of a man, but each of them had four faces and four wings. Their legs were straight; their feet were like those of a calf and gleamed like burnished bronze. Under their wings on four sides they had the hands of a man. All of them had faces and wings, and their wings touched one another. Each one went straight ahead; they did not turn as they moved.

— Ezekiel 1:4-9

The five hundred years after Samuel were a time of great prophets (Elijah, Elisha, Jonah, Amos, Hosea) and great kings (Saul, David, and Solomon). It was also the time of the division of the kingdom between the North (Israel) and the South (Judea), the fall of the Northern Kingdom, and, finally, the fall of Jerusalem itself.

Dreams are the Royal Road to the unconscious.

SIGMUND FREUD

Ezekiel's dream/vision appeared to the seventh century BCE Prophet in a time of international upheaval. The Assyrian Empire had begun to crumble at the hands of the Babylonians resulting in the exile of the Israelites from Jerusalem to Babylonia. Ezekiel's vision comes straight out of what Carl Jung calls the collective unconscious. The **collective unconscious** is a deeper unconscious than the personal unconscious. If this dream were coming out of the personal unconscious, the dreamer would know everyone and everything in the dream or vision. However, when there are figures that are part animal, part human, or anything the dreamer does not know in waking life, that is a sign that this vision or dream is coming from the collective unconscious.

The collective unconscious contains things we have not known in waking life. This knowledge comes from around the world and from throughout history. It is difficult to believe in the reality of the collective unconscious until one experiences it, particularly for those of us having grown up with a Western mindset.

Ezekiel had never known the likes of these "four living creatures" that are appearing in his vision. These creatures are what Jung calls "archetypes," universal images that come out of the collective unconscious.
Ezekiel continues:

> *Their faces looked like this: each of the four had the face of a man, and on the right side each had the face of a lion, and on the left the face of an ox; each also had the face of an eagle. Such were their faces. Their wings were spread out upward; each had two*

wings, one touching the wing of another creature on either side, and two wings covering the body. Each one went straight ahead. Wherever the spirit would go, they would go, without turning as they went. The appearance of the living creatures was like burning coals of fire or like torches. Fire moved back and forth among the creatures; it was bright, and lightning flashed out of it. The creatures sped back and forth like flashing lightning.

Get the picture? Actually, stop reading. Go back and reread the vision and see if you can imagine the picture of the four living creatures in your mind. Better still you may want to try to draw it. Get the picture in your imagination before reading further.

Have you ever seen the likes of this before? Neither had Ezekiel. Why? Because the language of the collective unconscious is metaphorical. Metaphor, as mentioned earlier, is one of the primary languages of the Divine. But what is this metaphor saying? To begin to understand this we need to hear the rest of the vision.

As I looked at the living creatures, I saw a wheel on the ground beside each creature with four faces. This was the appearance and structure of the wheels: They sparkled like chrysolite (a stone that appears in priestly breastplates), and all four looked alike. Each appeared to be like a wheel intersecting a wheel. As they moved, they would go in any one of four directions the creatures faced; the wheels did not turn about as the creatures went. Their rims were high and awesome, and all four rims were full of eyes all around. When the living creatures moved, the wheels beside them moved; and when the living creatures rose from the ground, the wheels rose.

Now the four living creatures are in motion. They have wheels. They are on the move. Stop before going further to get this picture in your imagination.

Notice that this dream/vision is becoming numinous, the beginning of a feeling of holiness: "Wherever the spirit would go, they would go, and the wheels would rise along with them, because the spirit of the living creatures was in the wheels."

> *When the creatures moved, I heard the sound of their wings, like the roar of rushing waters, like the voice of The Almighty, like the tumult of an army ... Then there came a voice from above the expanse over their heads as they stood with lowered wings. Above the expanse over their heads was what looked like a throne of sapphire and high above on the throne was a figure like that of a man. I saw that from what appeared to be his waist up he looked like glowing metal, as if full of fire, and that from there down he looked like fire; and brilliant light surrounded him. Like the appearance of a rainbow in the clouds on a rainy day, so was the radiance around him.*

This vision, this picture, this dream is bursting with a most powerful message: "God is no longer limited to the temple in Jerusalem." The Jews are in exile. They think God is back there in the Holy of Holies of the temple. One of the messages of this numinous vision/dream is that God is a moveable God, no longer limited to the temple. God has wheels. The four living creatures can move in all directions. This Divine presence can be experienced anywhere and at anytime through visions, dreams, and meditative states. Ezekiel, John-the-Baptist, and Jesus were all aware of this accessibility to the Divine. What a powerful message. And, just at the time when those in exile from Jerusalem need to hear it. Because it comes in the form of a vision/dream, it is all the more powerful, filled with the presence of the Divine.

I have been using the word "vision" and "dream" interchangeably. A vision is a dream that comes to us while awake and a dream is a vision that comes to us while we are asleep. They both come from the same place:

the unconscious — both the personal and the collective unconscious.

But are dreams such as Ezekiel's possible in our own lives? Indeed they are.

Consider the dream of Ruth Hoss, the mother of dream researcher and author Robert Hoss, a dream he describes in his book *Dream Language* (Innersource 2005). Ruth was in her 50's and, like Ezekiel, she was on a spiritual search for the meaning of life and death. Here is what she recorded in her dream journal:

Soul thrives as we jot down a thought in our diary or note a dream, and give body to a slight influx of eternity.

Thomas Moore

> *I saw a wheel of fire – a strange wheel endlessly turning. Fire – yet not fire – not material fire; electrical forces like the fire seen through closed eyes. The wheel was the Wheel of Time, and hovering above it were souls of all things created: animals, vegetables and man. Much like a computer, programmed to accept each one in time, each one descended onto the earth only when an opening appeared in the wheel. The vibrations at the opening were attuned to the vibrations of that particular soul. The return from earth happened in a similar manner. Only when the proper opening appeared and the vibrations were right could the soul return from whence it came. There were some who wandered or floated beneath the wheel, unable to return through fire until the proper opening appeared. And I saw the wheel from above, without wonder, as something I had seen before and recognized.*

Sounds like Ezekiel, doesn't it? Minus the computer analogy, that is. Many people have all kinds of archetypical figures rising up out of their dreams. Sometimes the dreams are so numinous the best we can do is simply stand in awe of them and let their numinosity work its way with us. Other times we find it helpful to do active imagination with different figures in the dream. A simple way to do this is to have a dialogue with a figure from our dream. Begin by

*How grateful I am to you
for loving in me something
which I thought I had entirely
lost, and someone who, I
thought, had long ago ceased
to be ... Dearest Proverb, I
love your name, its mystery,
its simplicity and its secret,
which even you yourself seem
not to appreciate.*

THOMAS MERTON

*The further I advance into
solitude the more clearly I see
the goodness of all things.*

THOMAS MERTON

saying "who are you and what are you doing in my dream?"
And see where the conversation takes you.

Dreams from the collective unconscious can seem very
strange. A friend had a dream that her right eye was
normal, but her left eye was an aquarium with seaweed
rippling in the water and the little fish swimming to and
fro. In another dream about the same time her left leg was
a slice of a watermelon. Now, those are strange dreams.
In responding to the question, "What is an aquarium to
you?" she said, "Things are not where they belong." She
answered the same for the slice of watermelon in place
of her left leg. When asked what was going on in her life
at the time she had this dream, she suddenly realized she
was in the wrong place. She was not where she belonged.
Her life was in the wrong place. Because of this dream
she changed directions in her life, put things where they
belonged. Dreams from the collective unconscious can
seem very odd, but they normally have an important
message for us. ◉

 ## Unlock One of Your Dreams

- What weird figures and things have occurred in your dreams?
- What things, that you have never seen before in waking life, have appeared in your dreams? Spend a few minutes recalling them and writing them down.

Unlock One of Your Dreams

 **Unlock One of Your Dreams**

- Now pick one of them to dialogue with as suggested above. As you dialogue on paper or with two chairs, see what insights pop up for you. If it is not something appropriate to dialogue with, circumambulate (walk around) it. Ask questions. Make associations. Record your insights.

Unlock One of Your Dreams

 ## Unlock One of Your Dreams

- **Archetypical** dreams are good ones to work in a group because you have a much larger source of symbolic knowledge gathered there. Or get out a good dream dictionary; look up some of the archetypical things/figures in your dream; and see if you have an "aha" with any of them. Write down any "ahas" here.

 **Unlock One of Your Dreams**

- Use anything you have learned so far to try to unlock this dream.
- Do any of the earlier learnings apply to this dream?
- Are the energies in the dream personal or collective?
- Is there any person or thing in the dream you need to confront and dialogue with to get more insight?

Unlock One of Your Dreams

It is important to record your dreams in the next few days because what you missed will show up in future dreams. The dream maker keeps sending dreams until we get the message. If you got it, the dream maker will not send another dream about that particular issue. Dreams tell us only what we don't know. We are not through with this dream. We have just begun.

- Does anything you have learned in this chapter give you additional insights into the dreams you worked in the previous chapters? Go back and write it down.
- In the following chapters you will be learning more about dreams. As you do, you will be revisiting this dream with your new knowledge. Write it down here.

Unlock One of Your Dreams

The chart below will help re-enforce some of the definitions we will continue to explore throughout the book.

Jungian Terminology

The most concise and accessible definition of **Jungian psychology** is that it is the dialogue between the conscious and the unconscious.

The **conscious** is everything we are aware of in waking life. Jung's **personal unconscious** is what Freud meant by the subconscious. It contains things we once knew, but have repressed. For Freud that was the totality of the unconscious. Jung expanded the understanding of the unconscious to the **collective unconscious** and pointed to evidence for its existence. The collective unconscious is the universal storehouse of symbols and history that everyone shares.

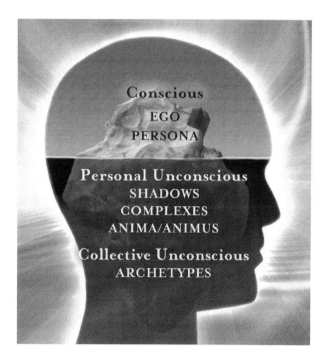

The **ego** and the **persona** are found in the conscious aspect of the individual. **Shadows** and **Anima/Animus** are found in the personal unconscious. The Anima/Animus acts as bridges to the collective unconscious. **Complexes** are in the personal unconscious but with an archetypical center connecting it to the collective unconscious. **Archetypes** are found in the collective unconscious.

For additional and more detailed definitions of Jungian terms see appendix E.

Chapter VIII

NEBUCHADNEZZAR'S TROUBLING DREAMS

King Nebuchadnezzar asked the prophet Daniel, 'Are you able to tell me what I saw in my dream and interpret it?'

— Daniel 2:26

Reason has little impact on complexes ... dreams provide direct access to the complexes.

ANTHONY STEVENS

Daniel, a contemporary of Ezekiel, was also a product of the exile. King Nebuchadnezzar had trained some young Israelites, including Daniel, in the Babylonian culture and language in order for them to serve in his court. Nebuchadnezzar tells Daniel that his dreams are waking him up at night. He has insomnia. He can't go back to sleep. Not only is he having insomnia, but he can't remember many details of his dreams, much less interpret them. But the part of the dream Nebuchadnezzar does remember troubles him greatly.

After working with Daniel on this dream, Nebuchadnezzar starts remembering more details of his dreams. So much so that he tells Daniel every detail of his next dream.

He tells Daniel the dream of the tree that was so tall its top touched the sky. It had beautiful leaves with abundant fruit and food for all. Under the tree "the beasts of the field found shelter, and the birds of the air lived in its branches; from it every creature was fed." Then, all of a sudden, before him in his dream was "a messenger, a holy one, coming down from heaven. He called in a loud voice: 'Cut down the tree and trim off its branches; strip off the leaves and scatter its fruit. Let the animals flee from under it and the birds from its branches. But let the stump and its roots, bound with iron and bronze, remain in the ground, in the grass of the field.'"

The dream continues, "Let him be drenched with the dew of heaven, and let him live with the animals among the plants of the earth. Let his mind be changed from that of a man and let him be given the mind of an animal, till seven times pass for him."

"This is the dream I, King Nebuchadnezzar, had. Now, Daniel, tell me what it means." Daniel did not answer him right away. In fact Daniel was "greatly perplexed for a time, and his thoughts terrified him."

When Daniel finally spoke about the dream, he said something startling: "You, O King, are the tree!" You are the tree. Wow. That insight opens up the whole dream, reminding us that everything in the dream is an aspect of the dreamer. Was Daniel the original gestalt therapist? I can just hear Daniel saying to Nebuchadnezzar,

> *You have become great and strong, but you will be cut down, driven away from people and live like wild animals. But the stump is saved, your kingdom will be restored to you when you acknowledge that heaven rules.*

This is a compensatory dream. Jung claims that many dreams have a compensatory element. Compensatory dreams balance us out. In this case the king has become too inflated and prideful. So, this dream humbles him. It balances him out. Alcoholics often have compensatory dreams. Shortly after they join AA many have what are known as "drunk dreams." They dream that they are drinking again and it scares them to death. What is happening is that they have put exaggerated energies towards not drinking, so, in their dreams, they are drinking. Often these dreamers try to repress such dreams when in reality the dreams are a good sign. They are compensatory.

Whenever I get too task oriented, a young girl will come in my dreams and make love to me. Now, this is pleasurable, but it also reminds me that, in waking life, I am not relating enough to others or taking the time to "smell the roses." This compensatory dream helps me to become aware. If I am not aware I just continue on unconsciously. That is why it is always helpful, when looking at a dream, to consider the dream's opposite. The dream may be telling us what is missing in our waking life. If we will listen to compensatory dreams we can sometimes avoid more tragic things happening in waking life. We can correct things while there is still time.

A Presbyterian minister from Texas, who at the time was a young single mother, had a troubling dream. She dreamed that she and her young daughter were in line at Auschwitz. She could see the smoke stacks over the hill. Then she noticed the line divided into two lines up ahead. She suddenly realized that they were sending the children to the right and the adults to the left and that she had only 10 minutes to tell her daughter everything she wanted to tell her. She woke up terrified.

Later that day she was at the church and hurried home for a quick bite before hurrying back to the church for a funeral. As she was leaving home her daughter said, "Maybe I will have to die so you will pay attention to me." The dream popped back into her mind. She got the message. Right after the funeral she went to her Presbyterian authorities and said, "I am taking a year's leave. If you want to pay me, that is fine. If not, that is ok too. But I am going to be with my daughter this year." This was indeed a very troubling dream, a dream that also came in the service of healing and wholeness.

These types of dreams are good ones to work with using Robert Hoss' "Six Magic Questions" (*Dream Language*, Innersource, 2005). They are magic questions, gestalt in nature, that tend to unleash insights and "ahas." Let's imagine how Nebuchadnezzar might answer the six questions. He would first have to pick an object from his dream that had high energy for him, become the object and answer the questions. Let's suppose he picks the tree and begins to answer the six questions.

> 1) Who or what are you (describe yourself, perhaps how you feel, as that dream element): "I am the tree. I am tall and strong. People admire and look up at me"

> 2) What is your purpose or function (what do you do)? "My purpose is to be tall and strong and give people protection from the elements."

> 3) What do you like about being that dream element? "I like being admired and told how beautiful and helpful I am. I like my strength and power. "

If we accept our complexes, and struggle with them, they give us the means through which we work out our salvation, the salvation offered us.

ANN ULANOV

4) What do you dislike about being that dream element? "I dislike the feeling of loneliness. I don't like being chopped down. I feel as if my entire world is caving in. All I have been is no more. I will be looked down on. I will no longer have power."

5) What do you fear most as that dream element? "I fear losing my power."

6) What do you desire most as that dream element? "What I desire most is to be real, not separated out from others. Maybe my goodness was getting in the way and I needed to be brought low. I desire for the remnant to be real and to enjoy the journey." ✪

A way to get at a complex in a dream is to ask "where in your life have you experienced feelings like those released in this dream?"

ANTHONY STEVENS

Unlock One of Your Dreams

Your assignment is to answer the same six questions. Pick an image from one of your dreams. Become the image. Answer these questions with the first thing that comes to your mind.

Who or what are you (describe yourself, perhaps how you feel, as that dream element):

"I am _____

_____

_____ "

What is your purpose or function (what do you do)? "My purpose is _____

_____

_____ "

What do you like about being that dream element? "I like _____

_____

_____ "

What do you dislike about being that dream element? "I dislike _____

_____

_____ "

What do you fear most as that dream element? "I fear _____

_____

_____ "

6) What do you desire most as that dream element? "What I desire most is _____

_____

_____ "

 **Unlock One of Your Dreams**

• Write down the insights that have come to you.

 **Unlock One of Your Dreams**

- Do any of the earlier learnings apply to this dream?
- Are the energies in the dream personal or collective?
- Is there any person or thing in the dream you need to confront and dialogue with to get more insight? Use anything you have learned so far to try to unlock this dream.

 **Unlock One of Your Dreams**

Further thoughts:

Insomnia signifies a conflict between a person's conscious and unconscious world. So there is something the king knows in his unconscious self, but his conscious self is not letting that knowledge through. He is repressing it. In this case it is probably too troubling.

Many people in our generation do not remember their dreams, for a number of reasons; chief among them is the fact that our western scientific worldview does not allow for the reality of the dream. There are many things that can be helpful in increasing dream recall. The first is to have a dream journal by your bed and write down the dream as soon as you awake, even if it is two words. The second is to ask for dreams in your prayers before going to sleep. The third is to read dream books and become a part of a dream group. Over-the-counter medication like serotonin increases your dream memory as will vitamin B-12. If none of these work, drink four glasses of water before going to bed and you will wake up in the middle of a dream.

Nebuchadnezzar tells Daniel a series of dreams. The interwoveness and next step in a dream series are fascinating. For an excellent exploration of a dream series (actually two, a young man and a middle aged woman) see John Sanford's book *Dreams and Healing.*

Daniel also had dreams that helped him with interpreting Nebuchadnezzar's dreams. Many analysts, clergy, spiritual directors, and dream counselors experience this helpful phenomenon. These types of dreams are not only beneficial when helping others work with their dreams, but can also be most helpful in pastoral situations. I paid a pastoral visit to a family whose teenage daughter had just died. That night in my dream a black woman stood behind me as I sat in my chair in my church office. The black woman represents "soul" to me. The meaning of this dream hit me like a ton of bricks. It became so clear to me that I had not had a "soul" time with that family. So, I made a second visit and we cried together.

When asked to interpret Nebuchadnezzar's dream, Daniel first tells him "no wise man, enchanter, magician or diviner can explain to the king the mystery he has asked about, but there is a God in heaven who reveals mysteries." In other words, God, working through Daniel (and Nebuchadnezzar), will help reveal the mystery. You will recall that Joseph said the same thing to Pharaoh when working with Pharaoh's dreams. They both assert that God is the interpreter, and with this understanding, they are willing to be involved in the process. Dreams do not always come to tell us pleasant things. But even troubling dreams come in the service of healing and wholeness.

Chapter IX

THE ARCHANGEL GABRIEL: THE BRIDGE BETWEEN OLD AND NEW TESTAMENTS

Gabriel, tell this man the meaning of the dream.

— Daniel 8:16

The angel said to him, "Do not be afraid, Zachariah; your prayer has been answered. Your wife Elizabeth will bear you a son and you are to give him the name John … I am Gabriel. I stand in the presence of God …"

— Luke 1:13-19

An angel of the Lord appeared to him in a dream and said, "Joseph, son of David, do not be afraid …"

— Matthew 1:20

In the sixth month God sent the angel Gabriel to Nazareth, a town in Galilee, to a virgin pledged to be married to a man named Joseph…the angel said to her, "Do not be afraid. Mary … you will be with child and give birth to a son, and you are to give him the name Jesus."

— Luke 1:30-31

From Daniel to Jesus is a long time (500 years). It was a period of the restoration of Israel and Jerusalem. The first group of Israelites returned to Israel under Zenrubbabel, the second under Ezra, and the third under Nehemiah. Herod the Great becomes the ruler in Palestine, and Augustus becomes the emperor in Rome.

But there is someone who transcends those years. The **archetypical** archangel Gabriel appears in dreams and visions in both the Old and New Testaments. Archetypical figures can transcend time and space. Gabriel, who interprets Daniel's Old Testament dream, is the same one who announces the birth of John-the-Baptist and Jesus in New Testament times. He is much like Aesculapius who appears in dreams of those seeking healing in the Greek world or Philemon, a constant wisdom figure in Carl Jung's dreams.

The archangel Gabriel is a revealer and bringer of reassurance as well as interpreter of dreams. When he appears, one feels the graciousness and powerful purpose of the One who sent him. Zachariah, Joseph, and Mary all felt this awe. He keeps saying: "Do not be afraid." "Do not be afraid." "Do not be afraid." They, like we, fear anything unknown or out of the ordinary or outside our worldview or our understanding of time and space. They were startled, but knew his appearance was real. I have had many people tell me, when they dream of someone close to them who has died, "I know it was my mother; it was her; it was real." There are certain dreams we cannot begin to explain to a scientific mind, but we know they are real. Such was the stance of these ordinary people who took on extraordinary vocations. After Gabriel's nocturnal visit, each felt, "Someone is with me; I don't have to face this alone."

Zachariah, a priest of Abijah (one of the 24 divisions of Jewish priests since the time of David), was concerned that he and his wife were getting old and that they had no children because his wife, Elizabeth, was barren. While this situation was heavy on his mind, Zachariah, chosen by lot, went to serve as a priest before God in the temple. His duty was to keep the incense burning before the altar day and night. In the middle of the night, Gabriel appeared to him on the right side of the altar. Zachariah was startled and gripped with fear. The angel said to him,

> *Do not be afraid, Zachariah; your prayer has been heard. Your wife Elizabeth will bear a son and his name will be John. He will be a joy and delight to you, and many will rejoice because of his birth, for he will be great in the sight of the Lord. He is never to take wine or other fermented drink, and he will be filled with the Holy Spirit, even from birth. Many of the people of Israel will he bring back to the Lord their God.*
> — *Luke 1:13-16*

"Zachariah asked the angel, 'How can I be sure of this? I am an old man and my wife is well along in years.'" (How many times have we asked that of dreams: "How can I be sure of this?") "The angel answered, I am Gabriel. I stand in the presence of God, and I have been sent to speak to you and to tell you this good news. And now you will be silent and not able to speak until the day this happens, because you did not believe my words, which will come true at their proper time."

The people outside the Temple wondered why Zachariah was staying so long in the temple, and why, when he came out, he could not speak. He made signs to them and finally they understood that he had seen a vision, but they did not know what the vision was. When his duty was over, he went back home. And lo and behold, after several months, Elizabeth became pregnant. On the eighth day after the birth of the baby, the family and friends gathered for the circumcision ceremony. Everyone felt sure they would name the child Zachariah, after his father. But the silenced Zachariah asked for a writing tablet. He wrote, "His name is John." Immediately his mouth was opened and his tongue was loosed, and he began to speak, praising God. The neighbors were filled with awe, and throughout the hill country of Judea people were talking about these things."

Zachariah could not contain himself and broke out in song, what we now know as the Benedictus Dominus Deus, a Morning Prayer canticle (The Book of Common Prayer, page 92).

How do you respond when a dream has come true? Some want to dance. Some want to sing. Some want to write a poem. Some just stand in silent awe.

Joseph was worried because the woman he loved was pregnant, but he knew he had not known her, in the Biblical sense. He thought about breaking the engagement quietly in order to not disgrace her. That's when Gabriel appeared to him in a dream saying, "Joseph, son of David, do not be afraid to take Mary as your wife, because what is conceived in her is of the Holy Spirit. She will give birth to a son, and you are to give him the name Jesus, because he will save the people from their sins" (Matthew 1:20, 21). Once Joseph's initial fear was gone, he was probably even more afraid and confused, wondering what in the world was happening. Nobody was going to believe this. This is the way we feel after some of the "unreal" dreams we have. It is only in retrospect that we "believe" such dreams. And Wisdom tells us to keep these dreams to ourselves or share them only with understanding friends or trusted dream groups.

In the sixth month after John was born to Elizabeth and Zechariah, the angel Gabriel appeared to Mary saying, "Greetings, you are highly favored! The Lord is with you." Mary was troubled with these words and wondered what they meant. Then Gabriel uttered his oft-repeated initial words to put people at ease, "Do not be afraid." He went on to explain to her that she would have a child named Jesus who would be great and called "son of the most high." Mary asked, "How will this be since I am a virgin?" Gabriel answered, "The Holy Spirit will come upon you and the power of the most high will overshadow you. So, the holy one to be born will be called the Son of God."

Mary's answer was "Fiat," the Latin word for "Let it be done unto me." What a response! She is the archetype for being receptive to the Divine being born in us. Every time I see a portrayal of Mary, it moves me into my receptive mode and I feel the possibilities of the Divine being born in me.

I felt this receptivity very strongly on a labyrinth walk and follow-up dream at the Washington Cathedral. I had been struggling for several years and was now meeting with a consultant in Washington, DC to discern if I should risk founding what is now The Haden Institute. It was on the labyrinth that I said, "Yes, let it be done unto me." The actual words were "Jesus, let's do it." The dream that night was of a doctor and his wife giving me $4,000 for a baby crib for the Church. In the dream I said "I can get a baby crib much cheaper than $4,000." When I awoke I remembered that "four" was the number of wholeness, completeness and totality. So, $4,000 was really solid. That dream, more than the consultant or anyone's opinion, is what gave me the courage to take the risk and launch The Haden Institute. Subsequent events have proved that dream's truth. ◎

 **Unlock One of Your Dreams**

- Have you ever had a dream that was announcing something to you or that was reassuring to you or that called you to a receptive mode? Have you ever had a dream that you answered "yes" to? What was it? Write the dream down.
- Circumambulate (walk around) it. What was it announcing to you or asking of you? How did you respond? What has happened in your life since then? How did you or how can you honor the dream?

 **Unlock One of Your Dreams**

 **Unlock One of Your Dreams**

- Have you ever had a dream in which you felt the presence of the Divine? Allow yourself to feel it again as you recall it here.

 **Unlock One of Your Dreams**

Unlock One of Your Dreams

- Use anything you have learned so far to try to unlock this dream.
- Do any of the earlier learnings apply to this dream?
- Are the energies in the dream personal or collective?
- Is there any person or thing in the dream you need to confront and dialogue with to get more insight?
- Use the "six magic questions" with this dream.

 **Unlock One of Your Dreams**

Further thoughts:

It is interesting that Zechariah's dream tells him that John-the-Baptist is "never to take wine or other fermented drink." The message of the dream is not whether we should drink or not. John-the-Baptist was a mystic. Not just a mystic, but a wild one who wore sackcloth and ate locusts and wild honey. He was going to be wild enough and so filled with the Holy Spirit that drink would get in the way. Carl Jung said the same kind of thing to author and Jungian analyst Robert Johnson. Robert tells a dream of a gigantic snake coming out of a hole in a Buddha tree and chasing him. He ran as fast as he could, but the snake was right behind him. Finally, as he continued running, he made a circle with his arms on the right side of his body. The snake moved its head up into the circle and they ran together. When his Zurich Jung Institute analyst, Emma Jung, heard this dream, she did not help with the interpretation, but rather said to Robert, "You have an appointment with Carl at 9am tomorrow morning." It was at that appointment, after hearing the dream, that the non-directive Carl Jung became very directive and said, "Don't ever marry or belong to any organizations." He told Robert this for the same reason Gabriel told John-the-Baptist's father that John was not to drink strong wine. Robert Johnson, like John-the-Baptist, needed to avoid anything that might interfere with his deep mystical nature.

Chapter X

JESUS' DESERT VISIONS

At once the Spirit drove him out into the desert, and he was in the desert forty days, being tempted by Satan. He was with wild animals and the angels attended him.

— Mark 1:12-13

To Honor and accept one's own shadow is a profound spiritual discipline.

ROBERT JOHNSON

Jesus was a mystic. He was a spirit person.

The Spirit appeared mystically as a dove at his baptism. As soon as he was baptized, he was driven out into the desert – not for a day, but for 40 days and 40 nights. This type of mystical experience became a pattern which gave sustenance to his life. At key times in his life he would go off into the desert or up into the mountains to pray, a deeper form of prayer with fewer words and a richer inner experience - mystical experience. Jesus is in the lineage of Elijah the prophet who knew that if you drew aside for a while and became quiet, you would begin to hear a "still small voice." The psalmist shows familiarity with this mystical tradition in the 46th psalm: "Be still and know that I am God."

Mystical experience requires that one become quiet in order to hear and see things on a deeper, divine, mystical, metaphorical level. That is exactly what Jesus did, not only here at the beginning of his ministry, but with Peter, James and John on the Mount of Transfiguration in the middle of his ministry and in the Garden of Gethsemane towards the close of his earthly ministry. In all three instances he not only hears voices, but sees visions. But in order to hear and see he must first be quiet. The same is true of dreams. By going to sleep we are going to a quiet place, a very quiet place. When we turn off our everyday world, a whole other world is turned on.

Immediately after his baptism Jesus goes to the desert. What happens in the desert?

Honi, the circle maker knew what happens in the desert. We are told by Flavius Josephus, a Jewish historian contemporary to the time of Jesus, that Honi was an assistant to those who went on retreat in the desert. It was Honi's task to draw a gigantic circle in the sand and make sure the person on retreat stayed in that circle for 40 days and 40 nights. Honi, or someone like him, most likely drew the circle in the desert for Jesus. Everyone going on retreat needs someone or some structure to keep them there –

even, and more especially, when the demons come, as they are sure to do.

So, what happened on Jesus' retreat?

After a prolonged time in the desert Jesus, like most people on retreat, begins to see things he did not ordinarily see. The dream-like figure Jesus sees is Satan. Satan causes Jesus to look at three shadow sides of himself that are likely to cause him trouble if he does not acknowledge and make friends with them. The three shadows are his temptation to miracle, power and magic.

Confronting the shadow precedes access to the transpersonal.

JEREMY TAYLOR

Miracle

> *Satan said to him, 'If you are the Son of God, tell this stone to become bread.' Jesus answered, 'People do not live on bread alone.'*
> *— Luke 4:3-4*

This encounter illustrates Jesus' temptation to use miraculous powers. He could carry out his mission much more easily if he would just change things by miracle. It would do the trick in the short run, but not the long run. Not using miracles to change things is certainly slower, but more authentic and in line with his mission. Jesus knew that people do not live on bread alone. They need inner/ spiritual sustenance as well.

Power

Since that didn't work, Satan tries again.

> *Satan led Jesus up to a high place and showed him the kingdoms of the world. And Satan said to him, 'I will give you all their authority and splendor, for it has been given to me, and I can give it to anyone I want to. So, if you worship me, it will be all yours.' Jesus answers, 'It is written: Worship the Lord your God and serve Him only.'*
> *— Luke 4:5-8*

This moment represents Jesus' temptation to power. Jesus

could have carried out his mission much more easily by
using his worldly powers. It is easier just to command
people what to do and how to act than it is to deal with
them in such a way that they, themselves, choose the right
way. He knows he must allow people to go through their
own process and struggle to become single-focused on
God's ways.

Magic

Finally, Satan led Jesus to Jerusalem and had him stand on
the highest point of the temple. "'If you are the Son of God,'
he said, 'Throw yourself from here. Your angels will
catch you.'"

> *Jesus answered, 'It is written: Do not put the Lord
> your God to the test.'*
> — *Luke 4:9-11*

Thus Jesus' temptation to magic has been brought to
consciousness. It is, indeed, easier to do things magically.
But had Jesus carried out his mission this way, it would
have denied the core of his mission.

Jesus, wisely, stops his life, pulls aside, and deals with these
three shadow aspects of himself before setting out on his
mission.

The same is true of us. If we do not deal with our shadows,
they will deal with us. Robert Johnson urges us to "make
friends with our shadow." That does not mean that we
have to act out our shadow. If everyone acted out their
negative shadows, there would be a lot of additional murder,
rape and illicit activity going on in the world.

In making friends with our shadow it is helpful to ask
four questions:

    1) Is it legal?
    2) Could it endanger my life?
    3) How might it affect my loved ones?
    4) Could I live with the consequences?

It is interesting that Carl Jung defines sin as "the refusal to become conscious." And this sin not only affects us, but its unconscious ripples impact the world in which we live. Jung further starkly states one of the key principles of life: if we do not acknowledge our shadow, it is automatically projected onto society.

This dynamic was in full force with one of my shadows, of which I was totally unconscious. A particular vestry person was very manipulative. I got excessively angry at his manipulation. But, I had learned that when I get excessively angry, I need to question myself. In this case I asked myself, "How do I manipulate?" My immediate answer was, "I do not manipulate. It is a high quality with me. I would never manipulate."After asking several more times I suddenly realized that I am very sophisticated in how I manipulate. As soon as I admitted that, the energy level between me and the vestry person was lowered. Although he did not quit manipulating altogether, his manipulating lessoned and so did my reaction to it.

My not being conscious of my shadow meant that it was automatically projected onto others causing their own negative activity to intensify.

Jesus states this dynamic so clearly: "Take the log out of your own eye before you take the speck out of your neighbor's eye and you will see clearly how to take the speck out of your neighbor's eye." (Matthew 7:3)

Being aware of our exaggerated feelings and asking the appropriate question is one way to recognize and work with our shadows. Another way is to notice the shadow figures that occur in our visions and dreams. That's what Jesus did.

The person of your same sex in your dream is often one of your shadows. The way to work with this phenomenon is to ask what the person is like; and then to ask how you are like that. Shadows can also appear in dreams in the form of animals and objects, even a blob on the bed. If you do

active imagination by dialoguing with the animal, object or person, insights and consciousness occur. This self-knowledge is usually self-motivating.

There are also **bright shadows**. For example: I projected my bright shadow onto Carl Jung for years. He was my hero. I admired him a lot. Gradually I began to withdraw my projection and recognize, accept and live the qualities in me that were Jung-like. Projection is good in the sense that we have to see things in projected form before we recognize them inside of ourselves. We can discover some of our bright shadows by naming our heroes or heroines and identifying what it is about our heroes that we really like and admire. Then ask, "where are those qualities in me?" Our bright shadows also appear in our dreams, usually in the form of someone or something we admire.

Shadow work is some of the most ethical and spiritual work we can do.

The Gospel of Mark ends this Jesus-in-the-wilderness pericope by saying, *"He was with wild animals and the angels attended him."*

Animals are very instinctual as illustrated by the donkey in the story of the Prophet Balaam (Num. 22). The donkey three times darted off the road. He knew that danger was ahead, but Balaam did not sense it. The donkey (like most animals) can sense when something is wrong long before people see it. Animals are instinctual. Some analysts have a dog in their therapy room and they watch the dog's reaction as people come into their counseling room. One therapist's dog once walked out when the client walked in. The analyst recounted that she realized later that she should have walked out also. Animals often appear in our dreams representing, metaphorically, our instinctual feelings.

The angels also ministered to Jesus. Many people tell of dreams where angels come to their aid. In such dreams we are transported to another world where we feel at home, where we are respected, where we are free and in harmony

with ourselves, our neighbors, the world, and the Divine.
Such dreams bring about a deeper healing in us than just
talking about our problems. This is the at-oneness state
Jesus found himself in after doing his shadow work. ⊙

Unlock One of Your Dreams

- Write down some of the people of the same sex that have appeared in your recent dreams.
- Take three of them and ask, "What are they like? What are their personalities like? What characteristic ways of acting stick out?" Write down the first thing that comes to your mind.
- Then go back and ask of each one, "How or where in my life am I like that?" Give time for the "ahas" to surface and then write them down. Hopefully you will be discovering some aspects of your shadow self.

Unlock One of Your Dreams

 **Unlock One of Your Dreams**

- Think of a person you hate or tend to get excessively angry with when their name comes to mind or they are in the same room. Write the person's name or initials down.
- Try to figure out what specifically you hate about them. Write it down.
- Then ask yourself, "Where am I like that?" You may have to ask the question several times before the truth surfaces. When it does emerge, write it down.

Unlock One of Your Dreams

- Who are your heroes? Write down the names of three of your heroes.
- What is it about each of them that makes them a hero for you? Where do you find that characteristic in yourself, a characteristic you may have repressed or denied? Write it down. You are discovering your Bright Shadow.

 **Unlock One of Your Dreams**

- What animals have appeared in your dreams? Write down the name of the animal.
- What emotions does each of those animals evoke in you? Write it down.
- Where have you found this feeling in yourself? To enhance your own insights into the animals in your dreams, you might want to do further research on those particular animals. Two suggested resource books are: 1) Andrews, Ted. *Animal Speak: The Spiritual and Magical Powers of Creatures Great and Small* (Winston Allen, illustrator; Margaret K. Andrews, photographer). 2) Chevalier, Jean & Gheerbrandt, Alain. *The Dictionary of Symbols.*

 **Unlock One of Your Dreams**

- Use anything you have learned so far to try to unlock this dream.
- Do any of the earlier learnings apply to this dream?
- Are the energies in the dream personal or collective?
- Is there any person or thing in the dream you need to confront and dialogue with to get more insight?
- Use the "six magic questions" with this dream.

Chapter XI

PILATE'S WIFE'S DREAM: DREAMING FOR OTHERS

While Pilate was sitting on the judge's seat, his wife sent him this message: "Don't have anything to do with that innocent man, for I have suffered a great deal today in a dream because of him."

— Matthew 27:19

Pilate was the Roman Procurator in Judea and the judge in the trial and execution of Jesus. While the trial was going on, Pilate's wife had a disturbing dream about Jesus. She sent word to Pilate to "have nothing to do with that innocent man." That's all we know about her and her dream. Matthew doesn't even give us her name, but from extracanonical writings we have learned her name was Procula.

Procula is in a long line of people who dream for others. Sometimes messages for a wife or husband or child may come for us through another family member's dream. Sometimes a person will have a dream for the group. This happened when I was conducting a dream weekend for 75 members of a church. When we started working a member's dream it became evident that her dream was for the whole congregation. She dreamed that her Rector was at their historic mother church taking people on tour of the church grounds. When he came to the front door of the church he said, "You will have to go on your own now. I can guide you no further." I learned later that the Rector was retiring in three months. So, of course, the congregation were now going to have to depend upon (and raise up) their own lay leader/guides. How affirming and unifying it was for a dream to declare this. Can you imagine churches listening for dreams to guide them? They would, of course, need to know the dream world and be discerning with their dreams. But attending to their dreams would be deeply unifying, motivating and spiritually uplifting.

Robert Van de Castle, dream researcher at the University of Virginia and author of the classic *Our Dreaming Mind*, has developed what he calls the "Dream Helper Ceremony." Before going to bed the dream helpers gather around the target person in a bonding ceremony (praying, singing, drumming, meditating or just silently holding hands). The target person does not share or even hint at the problem for which he or she is seeking guidance. The dreamers vow to devote their dream this one night to the target person rather than to themselves. The next morning when the group gathers, the dream helpers share their dreams and then the target person shares the problem for which he or she was seeking guidance. The group then looks for correlations. They are usually amazed and surprised at what the dreams have revealed.

The dream helpers in one of Van de Castle's ceremonies reported the following: a black car driving into the town of White Hall, an Oreo cookie, a scoop of chocolate and vanilla ice cream, black and white keys on a piano, Martin Luther King preaching in front of the White House. The target person then shared the problem she needed guidance with: she (a white person) was dating a black person and struggling with the negative reaction she expected from her family. In addition, one dream helper dreamed that his watch was slow. Another dreamed of seeing a movie in slow motion. So, they counseled her to "go slow" in talking to her parents until she was sure of the relationship with this man.

During one of Robert Van de Castle's dream helper ceremonies the crowd was so large he divided it into two groups. Robert led one group and I took the other. We had similar results as those just described, but there was no relation between the dreams of the two groups. The dreams reported in my group were right on target with the target person's concern, but not related at all to the target person in Robert's group and vice versa. Also no dream in either group grasped the full significance of the target dreamer's concern. Each dream had a common thread, but different commentary. The dreams of the whole group were needed.

The purpose of this ceremony is not to 'wow' people (though it does), but rather for all to be a part of the healing process. It is a clear demonstration of the telepathy that travels from person to person in the dream world. Van de Castle claims that if a large number of people were ever to agree to use the power of the dreaming mind to help each other, we would witness a dramatic change in planetary consciousness.

There is a lovely image of dream sharing in Dorothy Bryant's book, *The Kin of Atta Are Waiting for You.* One of the Kin of Atta's traditions is for each family to sleep in a circle each night with their heads in the center. The first thing they do in the morning is to share their dreams. They make decisions for the day in the light of the family's nightly dreams. There is a tribe that practices this ritual with the whole tribe each day. There are families in our day and time who share their dreams when they wake up. Doing so enriches their life and deepens their bond with one another.

Many dreams, like Procula's, surround public events. There were a large number of pre 9/11 dreams. An old man in Afghanistan told Osama Ben Laden shortly after 9/11 that his nephew dreamed of a plane hitting a tall building. Osama responded, "Yes, I know. We knew we could keep a secret but we were afraid that it would get out in the dream world." His culture knows the reality of the dream world as do all religions and cultures excluding, unfortunately, Western religions and cultures. It is interesting that when the Eastern and Western Christian church split, the East preserved phenomena like dreams, Icons, the Jesus breath prayer, and other things of a mystical nature. Those cultures know the reality of the dream world and the mystical world. We in the West have been one-sided for so long that we now have a deep hunger for the mystical. Immersing ourselves in the dream world can be a channel to the mystical realm where once again we can "know" the Divine Presence. As Carl Jung said when asked by a BBC commentator if he still believed in God, "Believe? That's hard to say. No, I do not believe. I know." ✪

Unlock One of Your Dreams

- Have you had a dream you felt was for another, or heard another's dream you felt was for you? Describe the dream and the situation involved.
- What discernment made you feel their dream was for you? Or that your dream was for others?

 **Unlock One of Your Dreams**

Unlock One of Your Dreams

Have you ever deliberately dreamed for others? Been a dream helper? Would you like to experience a dream helper ceremony? If so, do it only with a mature dream group following the Dream Helper Ceremony guidelines. The guidelines are as follows:

- The dream group leader asks for a volunteer to be the target person.

- The target person writes on a piece of paper the concern for which she or he is seeking guidance, something serious and genuine.

- The target person does not share her concern with the group, but rather keeps the paper to herself.

- The target person passes around an item of hers (a bracelet, a watch, a scarf, etc.) so the group can pick up the target person's energy.

- The group gathers around the target person in a bonding ceremony (praying, singing, drumming, chanting, meditating, lighting a candle or just silently holding hands).

- The dream helpers go to sleep with the intention of dreaming for the target person.

- The dream helpers write down their dreams as soon as they awake.

- The dream group gathers and the dream helpers each share their dreams of the previous night without further comment.

- The target person then shares the concern for which she is seeking guidance.

- The group leader guides a discussion of the correlations, insights and guidance from the dreams.

- The group, including the target person, comments on what this process has meant to them.

- The dream group closes with a ritual of thanksgiving to the Giver of the dream with its resultant guidance and prays for the healing of this broken world and for the wider exposure to the unopened letters from God available to us every night.

Anyone who wants to learn more about this method can attend The Haden Institute Summer Dream Conference (www.hadeninstitute.com) or the annual International Association for the Study of Dreams Conference (www.asdreams.org).

Unlock One of Your Dreams

Chapter XII

PAUL, BLINDED BY THE LIGHT
HEARS A VOICE

*Meanwhile, Saul was still breathing out murderous threats
against the Lord's disciples. He went to the high priest and asked
him for letters to the synagogue in Damascus, so that if he found
any there who belonged to the Way, whether men or women,
he might take them as prisoners to Jerusalem. As he neared
Damascus on his journey, suddenly a light from Heaven flashed
around him. He fell to the ground and heard a voice say to him,
'Saul, Saul why do you persecute me?'*

'Who are you, Lord?' Saul said.

*'I am Jesus whom you are persecuting,' he replied. 'Now get up
and go into the city and you will be told what to do.'*

*The men traveling with Saul stood there speechless; they heard
the sound but did not see anyone. Saul got up from the ground,
but when he opened his eyes he could see nothing. So they led
him by the hand into Damascus. For three days he was blind,
and did not drink or eat anything.*

— Acts 9:1-9

THE
HADEN
INSTITUTE

Conversion is a wonderful and amazing thing. People who have the most exaggerated conversion experience are the ones who have wandered far in the opposite direction. They, usually, have to be hit by lightning to wake up to the truth.

Such was the case with Paul. He was at the stoning of Steven, one of the stalwarts of Christianity, approving this horrendous act. And now "still breathing murderous threats towards the Lord's Disciples" he was on his way to Damascus to capture Christians and bring them to Jerusalem to incarcerate them.

I cannot understand my own
behavior.

ST. PAUL

On the way to Damascus he was hit by lightning: "a light from heaven flashed around him."

And then Saul heard a voice:
>"Saul, Saul why do you persecute me?"
>"Who are you?"
>"I am Jesus. "
In that moment Saul was converted.

There is in all visible things
an invisible fecundity,
a dimmed light, a meek
namelessness, a hidden
wholeness. This mysterious
Unity and Integrity is
Wisdom, the Mother of all,
Natura naturans.

THOMAS MERTON

He fell to his knees, awe-struck, dumbfounded. He could not move.

When he opened his eyes, he realized he could not see. Blinded by the light for three days, he did not eat or drink. His companions had to lead him by the hand.

In a daze, he moved, as instructed, towards Damascus, not knowing what was going to happen there. He now, like Abraham, had faith, moving out, not knowing where he was going, but comfortable in the feeling he was being led by God.

Meanwhile in Damascus, a man named Ananias was also having visions. In the vision God was telling Ananias to go to Judas's house on Straight Street and there he would meet a man from Tarsus named Saul. Ananias said: Wait a minute. Isn't he the one persecuting the Christians and coming to Damascus to get us? There is no way I am going to get anywhere near Saul.

But God assured him that Saul had changed, so much so that his name was about to be changed from "Saul" to "Paul." So Ananias went to Judas's house on Straight Street and laid his hands in healing prayer upon Paul's head. Paul's sight was restored. He was baptized and ceased capturing the Christians to imprison them in Jerusalem, soon he began to share his conversion experience in Damascus and preach in the synagogues that Jesus is Lord.

This conversion experience has been repeated throughout the centuries and often accompanied by a vision or a dream. Let me share three such conversion experiences, each of which is accompanied by a dream. The three are Constantine, 4th century Emperor of the Roman Empire; John Newton, slave ship captain and Anglican priest who authored the hymn "Amazing Grace;" and the son of the atheist Madelyn Murray O'Hare who became a Christian minister.

Constantine's Conversion Dream

Constantine had a vision and a dream surrounding his conversion in 313 CE. There are several versions of the vision and dream, but the earliest version is the one Constantine told to his son's tutor shortly after having the dream.

This is the dream Constantine's son's tutor reports: During the day Constantine saw the XP symbol in the sky. He wondered what it was. That night Jesus appeared in his dream with the XP symbol in his hand. XP, in Greek, is chi ro, the first two letters of Kristos, Christ. The dream took place the night before the famous battle of Milvian Bridge. Constantine put the XP symbol on his helmet and ordered all soldiers to put this symbol on their breast plates. The XP symbol remained on the Roman soldier's armor for more than nine hundred years. Think of that – a symbol from a dream displayed for over nine hundred years.

Yesterday, in Louisville, at the corner of 4th and Walnut, suddenly I realized that I loved all the people and that none of them were, or could be, totally alien to me; as if waking from a dream – the dream of my separateness, of my "special" vocation to be different. My vocation does not really make me different from the rest of men or just one in a special category, except artificially, juridically. I am still a member of the human race – and what more glorious destiny is there for man, since the Word was made flesh and became, too, a member of the human race.

THOMAS MERTON

And more importantly, 300 years of Christian persecution ends, the Roman Emperor encourages the Christian faith, the council of Nicaea produces a common creed, the building of churches increases in Jerusalem and throughout the empire, and Christianity begins to grow at a very fast rate. All of this resulting from a single dream.

The dark side is that Constantine, even after he was converted to Jesus Christ, had his wife and son put to death. His death-bed baptism was, in part, to ask forgiveness for this and other horrendous acts. So, conversion is a process that does not necessarily change an individual totally, or overnight. But it does produce change. Although much controversy rightly surrounds Constantine's effect on Christianity, one cannot deny his role in the growth of Christianity. Dreams are, indeed, more powerful than we know.

First take the log out of your own eye and you will then see clearly how to take the speck out of your neighbor's eye.

JESUS

John Newton's Conversion Dream

1600 years later a dream produced another conversion resulting in probably the most widely known and loved hymn of all time, "Amazing Grace." The hymn speaks of "a wretch like me." John Newton, the author, was a wretch. The captain of a slave ship, he kept slaves in chains in the bottom of the boat bringing them from Africa to England. Later he was ordained an Anglican Priest. Someone asked him what caused this change. He said it was a dream.

In the dream he is on board a ship in the Mediterranean Sea. A man comes on board and gives him a ring, telling him if he wears this ring he will always be doing the most important thing. John puts the ring on. A second man comes to him asking about the ring. John shares what happened and the second man tells him, "That's superstitious." John then throws the ring into the ocean. A third man, not unlike the first man, comes on board asking John why he is so sad. John tells him about the ring, then adds: "It seems like every good thing in life I throw away." Hearing this, the third man dives into the sea, gets the ring, and brings it back on board. John says, "Thank you. Let me put it on." The third man says, "No, I am going to hold it in safe keeping. Whenever you need it, call on me and two things will happen. You will develop a relationship with me and you will be doing the most important thing."

Since conversion is, indeed, a continuing process, John's total conversion did not happen overnight. John Newton's first conversion was a personal one to Jesus Christ. He gave up profanity, gambling, and drinking, but he continued to be a slave ship captain for three years. It was later in his life that he renounced the slave trade. But even in his retirement he continued to invest his money in Manesty's slaving operations. This story really makes the point that conversion, although it has its dynamic moments, is normally a continuing process.

Everything that irritates us about others can lead us to an understanding of ourselves.

C. G. JUNG

Madelyn Murray O'Hare's Son's Conversion Dream

The son of the famous atheist Madelyn Murray O'Hare had a conversion dream. As a child he was the object of the Supreme Court case concerning no prayer in school and was always told never to read the Bible. When he grew up, he became an ordained Christian minister with a special ministry to atheists. When asked how this conversion happened, he said it was a dream. In the dream a sword is pointing to an open Bible. On the handle of the sword are the Latin initials which mean "read this book." He began to read the Bible, was converted and ordained a Christian minister.

I wish there were archives of all of the conversions in history prompted by dreams. Many are not even recorded because of society's discounting dreams. But many are now resurfacing as we begin to honor the dream. ✿

 **Unlock One of Your Dreams**

- Conversions come in all degrees of energy; some are sudden, and some are developed over a longer period of time. What have been some of the conversions (changes in thoughts or ways of acting) in your life? Write them down.
- Were there any dreams associated with these conversion experiences? Write them down.

Unlock One of Your Dreams

 **Unlock One of Your Dreams**

- What other conversions have you heard in addition to the three mentioned above? Write them down.
- Were there dreams or visions associated with these conversion experiences? Write them down.

 **Unlock One of Your Dreams**

- Use anything you have learned so far to try to unlock this dream.
- Do any of the earlier learnings apply to this dream?
- Are the energies in the dream personal or collective?
- Is there any person or thing in the dream you need to confront and dialogue with to get more insight?
- Use the "six magic questions" with this dream.

Chapter XIII

PETER'S DREAM CHANGES CHRISTIANITY: COULD IT HAPPEN TODAY?

About noon the following day as they were on their journey and approaching the city, Peter went up on the roof to pray. He became hungry and wanted something to eat, and while the meal was being prepared, he fell into a trance. He saw heaven opened, and something like a large sheet being let down to earth by its four corners. It contained all kinds of four-footed animals, as well as reptiles of the earth and birds of the air. Then a voice told him, 'Get up, Peter. Kill and eat.' 'Surely not, Lord!' Peter replied. 'I have never eaten anything impure or unclean.' The voice spoke to him a second time, 'Do not call impure anything that God has made clean.' This happened three times, and immediately the sheet was taken back into heaven.

— Acts 10:9-16

The divisive issue in the early church was not homosexuality, women priests, or prayer book revision, but circumcision. Circumcision, the practice of cutting off the foreskin of the genital organ, was an act of cleanliness by people in the ancient near east. However, it took on an additional meaning for the Hebrews for whom it became an act of initiation into the covenant community. God told Abraham, "You shall be circumcised in the flesh of your foreskins, and it shall be to you a sign of the covenant between you and me." (Gen. 17:11) John the Baptist and Jesus and all good Jews of the day were circumcised on the eighth day after their birth.

Paul was circumcised and insisted on the circumcision of Timothy, son of a Jewish mother and a Greek father. But because Paul became the greatest missionary to the gentiles, he became adamant that gentiles did not need to be circumcised to become Christians. Peter, on the other hand, was adamantly for circumcision. That is, until he received his dream from God saying, metaphorically, it was ok to be uncircumcised and be baptized a Christian. Of course, Peter did not understand the dream at first because God speaks in metaphorical language in dreams, day-dreams and visions. This trance induced day-dream is about more than eating unclean animals. It is about that, but much more than that.

Peter had been taught all his life not to eat unclean animals, animals with a divided hoof and that chew their cud (like camels, rabbits and swine). Not eating unclean animals was part of Peter's religious heritage. God, in this day-dream, is telling Peter to do something totally against church law. God says, "Eat." Peter says, "I can't eat."

While Peter is pondering (circumambulating) this day-dream, three men come to his house to tell him that Cornelius, a gentile centurion, has dreamed about Peter. Peter is intrigued. So much so, that even though it was against the law for a Jew to associate with a gentile, he goes to Cornelius' house. God had also been speaking to Cornelius through his dreams. As he begins to talk to

Cornelius, Peter starts to realize how true it is that God does not show favoritism, but accepts everyone. Peter also begins to notice that the Holy Spirit is flowing through everyone there, not just the circumcised ones who have come with him. Both the circumcised and uncircumcised speak in tongues on this day at Cornelius' house. That does it. Peter asks himself and those assembled a rhetorical question: "Should anyone be denied baptism solely because he is uncircumcised?" His heart and theology have been changed by this dream and the resulting experience, so Peter orders that the uncircumcised be baptized in the name of Jesus Christ.

As you would expect, when Peter goes to church headquarters in Jerusalem he is criticized severely. But when he explains to James and the other church leaders how God spoke to him in a dream and the revelations that came to him as he was at Cornelius' house, they had no other objections. The rules got changed. They have been so ever since.

Islam's practice of praying five times a day came through a dream. It was a dream that converted John Newton from being a "wretched" slave ship captain to an Anglican priest and subsequently writing the beloved hymn "Amazing Grace."

Can similar things happen in our day? Indeed they can. Gandhi's non-violent protest (which Martin Luther King adopted) came through a dream. President Lyndon Johnson's dream changed history. It was the third in a series of three dreams. In the first dream he was on his Texas ranch tied to a chair with the cattle charging towards him. It was a nightmare. In the second dream he was working late at his vice-president's desk. He wanted to get up and quit work, but realized his legs were shackled to the chair. The third dream was the one that changed history. In this dream he was swimming across a river but could not get to the other side because he was caught in the current. He turned back, but could not return to shore. In fact he could not get to either shore. Upon awaking and circumambulating this dream it occurred to him that unless he got out of the presidency, the Vietnam War would not be solved. He, shortly thereafter, appeared on television and announced he would not run for a second term. Talk about honoring your dream! That's doing it in spades.

God's revelation through dreams can be a most powerful way Christians of opposing viewpoints can come together or, at least, cultivate respect for each other. Neither scripture text-proving nor strict dogma will do it. ✪

Unlock One of Your Dreams

- Peter was totally softened by his dream. Has your attitude ever been softened by a dream? Have you had dreams from God asking for a change in your life or shift in your theology? What was the dream? And what change was suggested? Write down the dream and the change that was asked for.

Unlock One of Your Dreams

 **Unlock One of Your Dreams**

- How can you help today's church with the recovery of the ancient wisdom of God speaking through our nightly dreams? Peter's dream demonstrates how life-changing and refreshing and uniting for the church this could be.

 **Unlock One of Your Dreams**

- Use anything you have learned so far to try to unlock this dream.
- Do any of the earlier learnings apply to this dream?
- Are the energies in the dream personal or collective?
- Is there any person or thing in the dream you need to confront and dialogue with to get more insight?
- Use the "six magic questions" with this dream.

Chapter XIV

THE REVELATION OF JOHN
AS A PROCESS OF INDIVIDUATION

I, John, your brother and companion in the suffering, and in the kingdom and the patient endurance that are ours in Jesus Christ, was on the isle of Patmos, for the word of God and for testimony of Jesus Christ. I was in the spirit on the Lord's day, and heard behind me a great voice, as of a trumpet, saying, "I am Alpha and Omega, the first and the last, write on a scroll what you see and send it to the seven churches in Asia."

— Revelation 1:9-11

Our dreams teach us what our own life-experiment is all about, what it means to live at this particular time in history, and about our ultimate origin and destination.

JOHN SANFORD

The Revelation of John is a classic of Christian literature. It is much like Dante's *Divine Comedy*. But it has long been a puzzle for many Christians. It must be studied, struggled with, and approached on a symbolic level. Only then does it begin to come to life for us all.

The Book of Revelation, like so much apocalyptic writing, was born out of innocent suffering. Jesus had been crucified. Rome was persecuting the Christians — literally throwing them to the lions, or cutting their heads off, or crucifying them. It would be like living in Iraq today, where the Christian church is about to vanish because of the persecutions and beheadings. In both incidences the Christians were and are being specifically targeted. John, the author of Revelation, was at the crucifixion of Jesus, but left Jerusalem and was living in Ephesus with Mary, the mother of Jesus. John, himself, was tortured by immersion in a boiling pot of oil and then banished to the Isle of Patmos in the Aegean Sea. It was on the Isle of Patmos that John had his dream-like vision.

As with all dreams and visions, there are multiple layers of meaning in this Apocalypse of John. Some see John's Revelation as speaking about events at the time (Nero persecuting the Christians). Others see it as foretelling future wars and catastrophes and the end of the world. Still others see it as describing a process, a process that is relevant to all times and all places and all people. Carl Jung calls it the process of individuation, the process of becoming what we are called to be. So, let us explore the Book of Revelation as a process of individuation.

Three Wars

There are three wars going on in the Book of Revelation: the war in heaven, the war on earth, and the war that's going on inside all of us. The Book of Revelation speaks of all three. The wars are between good and evil. We're fighting and struggling all the time with good and evil within ourselves. This world in which we live struggles with good and evil. And there's even a struggle between good and evil in the heavenly sphere, in the spiritual realm.

The Beast

The Book of Revelation is also about two powers. One is the power of the beast. The other is the power of the Lamb. The power of the beast is the power to control and manipulate. We all use that kind of power from time to time — in our home, in our work, in the world.

The power of the Lamb is the power of Christ, the sacrificial Lamb. It is the power to heal and to set free. When we use the power of the Lamb, our power sets people free and causes healing to happen. The Book of Revelation is about the conflict between those two kinds of power, the power of the beast and the power of the Lamb.

There are three beasts: the dragon in heaven, the beast from the sea, and the beast from the earth. Together they form a demonic trinity. You'll find with all these dragons and beasts, they are similar to the divine. But not quite. Evil likes to take on the image of the divine to sneak around and fool people in many ways. The Four Horsemen of the Apocalypse illustrates this, as well as going deeper into the individuation process.

The Four Horsemen of the Apocalypse

One of my favorite parts of John's vision is the Four Horsemen of the Apocalypse. There are four horses. One of them is white. One of them is red. One of them is black. And one of them is pale. The rider on the white horse has a bow and is wearing a crown. The rider on the red horse has a sword and produces much bloodshed. The rider on the black horse has the scales, the scales of economic systems which have gone awry. And finally, there is the pale horse, the horse that is ridden by death. That fourth horse is the power of death.

The white horse is almost a personification of Christ, but not quite. It's the way things always start out. These horses represent the whole system of how evil happens in our world. It starts out looking very, very good, like that white horse. Evil wears the mask of divinity a lot of times. Frequently you and I enter conflicts for various righteous reasons: to oppose oppression or evil; to defeat tyranny or to end war; to help the environment or to save the human race: all kinds of good causes.

We begin these causes on the white horse. But, pretty soon, the red horse comes along. The red horse is the blood horse. Even good and righteous causes, and good and righteous wars, can and do bring about bloodshed and destruction.

Then there's the black horse whose rider is holding the scales, a symbol of the economy gone awry. When the economy goes awry, famine, starvation, and economic enslavement ensue. This cycle repeats itself again and again throughout history.

Finally, there is the pale horse whose rider is Death, the final resting place of evil. Death — the ultimate power to control.

In the beginning, evil often seems enticing, attractive, desirable. No one knowingly wants to get caught in the clutches of the beast of evil. We're seduced into mounting that old horse.

The Lamb

The power of the Lamb is not to manipulate and control, but rather to heal and to set free. In the fifth chapter of Revelation we see the Lamb sitting on a throne surrounded by four living creatures. At the bottom left is a man. At the top left is a lion. At the top right is a calf. At the bottom right is an eagle. The early church designated these as Matthew, Mark, Luke, and John: the four gospels.

So, traditionally the man with six wings symbolizes Matthew; the lion symbolizes Mark; the calf, Luke; and the eagle, John. Surrounding those symbols on both sides are the twenty-four elders. In the middle, the great multitude from every nation and every race on earth praises the Lamb. This picture is a **mandala**, a symbol for wholeness in all cultures.

We also notice that the Lamb is the sacrificial Lamb. There is blood coming out of the Lamb. One of the elders is catching the blood in a chalice, symbolic of our taking the Eucharist, the body and the blood of the Lamb. The Lamb is certainly symbolic of Jesus, the sacrificial Lamb who died on the cross.

The symbol of the sacrificial Lamb carries us all the way back to Exodus when the Lamb was sacrificed, and the blood put over the door in X's, so the last plague would skip over those doors and not kill the oldest son. The Passover also represents the transition of the Israelites from slavery in Egypt to freedom in the Promised Land. This is another symbol of the Lamb, the freedom that the Lamb brings.

Both the Beast and the Lamb in the Book of Revelation have horns, signifying power and dominion. The Beast wears a crown on its horns, flouting its dominion. The Lamb's seven eyes never close, keeping a constant watch for injustice and oppression.

The Beast in the Book of Revelation represents pseudo-suffering. The Beast does, indeed, bear a wound. But it is the kind of wound meant to be seen, meant to attract the attention of others. On the other hand, the suffering of the Lamb is genuine and purposeful.

The power that is based on deceit will lose in the confrontation with the truth. We see it happen again and again. It may take years, or decades, but a power based on deceit will eventually crumble.

Inside the scroll is God's plan for salvation. The Lamb is the only one who can open up the scroll. That is, Jesus is the key to understanding God's new way. Jesus illustrated this new way at the meal when he, the Master, washed the disciples' feet then asked them to wash one another's feet. The power of the Lamb is servant leadership, not manipulative power moves.

The Power of the Beast manipulates and controls. The power of the Lamb heals and liberates.

The New Jerusalem

The New Jerusalem is the result of Lamb power put into action.

Chapters 21 and 22 of the Book of Revelation are a dream of the New Jerusalem. It is analogous to Jesus' dream of the Kingdom of God.

Jesus says many things about the Kingdom of God. It is the Kingdom of love, the Good Samaritan kind of love that stops, listens, and heals. Jesus' dream of the Kingdom and John's dream of the New Jerusalem are the same.

In 1963, Martin Luther King gave a speech in Washington, DC, of his dream - his own New Jerusalem.

> *I say to you today, my friends, that in spite of the difficulties and frustrations of the moment, I still have a dream. It is a dream deeply rooted in the American dream. I have a dream that one day this nation will rise up and live out the true meaning of its creed: 'We hold these truths to be self-evident – that all men are created equal.' I have a dream that one day on the red hills of Georgia, the sons of former slaves and the sons of former slave owners will be able to sit down together at the table of brotherhood.*
>
> *I have a dream that one day even the state of Mississippi, a desert state sweltering with the heat of injustice and oppression, will be transformed into an oasis of freedom and justice. I have a dream that my four little children will one day live in a nation where they will not be judged by the color of their skin but by the content of their character. I have a dream today. I have a dream that one day every valley shall be exalted, every hill and mountain shall be made low, the rough places will be made plains, and the crooked places will be made straight, and the glory of the Lord shall be revealed, and all flesh shall see it together.*

Martin Luther King's speech speaks of dissatisfaction with things of the past and the present, but then it takes that all important step of giving us a vision for the future. It is that vision that has pulled society towards justice rather than injustice.

The Book of Revelation speaks of the injustices. But, it doesn't stop there. It gives us a vision of the future: "Then I saw a new heaven and a new earth." Interesting, it's not just about a new heaven in the sky, by and by: "I saw a new Heaven and a new earth. And I saw a heavenly city, the New Jerusalem coming down out of heaven."

It is coming down to us. It's a new earthly vision. A pure gift "prepared as a bride beautifully dressed for her husband."

Just as Martin Luther King had a vision for this country, so John received a vision for all Christendom.

The Book of Revelation does tell us something about the first century and the persecutions Christians endured. It also tells us some things about the future in general terms. But, more importantly, it contains eternal truths relevant to our contemporary life. It teaches us to recognize evil as we see it, and to recognize demonic powers in ourselves and others. It urges us to begin to exercise the power of the Lamb, and to have that vision of the kind of world God desires for us.

John's vision helps us to see this journey as a definitive process; a process from beastly power to Lamb power to the New Jerusalem. It is the process of individuation, growth towards that to which God is calling us.

When we work with this vision as we work with a dream, allowing our imagination and inspiration to do its work, intuition flows. A river of "ahas" becomes a powerful, integrity-filled, healing force for our lives.

Thanks be to God for our dreams — those letters from the Lamb Who gives of Himself for us. ❂

The dream is the small hidden door in the innermost and most secret recesses of the soul, opening into that cosmic night which was psyche long before there was any ego-consciousness, and which will remain psyche no matter how far our ego-consciousness extends.

C. G. JUNG

Appendix A

THE HADEN INSTITUTE METHOD FOR WORKING WITH YOUR DREAMS INDIVIDUALLY

1. Write the dream in the first person in the center of the page with wide margins on both sides for notes. (An option is to use a separate page for notes if the dream is already written in your journal. When you write the dream in your journal, you may want to either write it in the middle of the page or write it on the left hand pages leaving the right hand pages blank for notes.)

2. What is the setting of the dream? In the upper left hand margin describe the setting. As the scenes change mark each with a Roman numeral. Give each separate scene its own title.

3. What is the feeling tone of the dream? Mark these feelings down in the left hand margin. How do you feel at the end of the dream?

4. What part of the dream has the highest energy for you? Mark it with an "E."

5. Circle all of the people in the dream. Draw a simple circle around people of the same sex (often your shadow) and a jagged circle around people of the opposite sex (your anima/animus). Draw a line from each one to the right margin and write down three words that describe each one. Then ask yourself, "Where am I like that?" Do this with each person. In describing what they are like, use the first thing that comes to your mind.

6. Put a square around any animals in the dream. Draw a line to the margin and write down the characteristics of that animal and the particular emotion the animal is projecting in your dream or what emotion you associate with that animal. Since it is an animal, the emotion will probably be on the instinctual level. See if you can become aware of those animal feelings within you. You may want to read up on that particular animal in nature and mythology books.

7. Underline the objects in the dream (like a house or a road). What personal associations do you have with that object? Again, ask what that object is

like and what its function is in the dream. Particularly note if it is odd in any way or doing something uncharacteristic. Remember that objects in dreams are also a part of you and ask yourself the question, "What part of me does that thing represent?"

8. Now verbalize the dream symbolically, i.e., "My anima and another anima aspect of myself and I were in a room with my shadow." Just by expressing it symbolically in Jungian terms, additional knowledge will probably pop into your head.

9. Where is the tension in the dream? For example are there conflicting emotions going on? Write down those conflicting emotions. Give each a name. Which one seems to be the "underdog" and which one seems to be the "overdog?" One way to dialogue with tension is to get the "underdog" and "overdog" in dialogue with each other. You can do this in a journaling fashion starting with the "underdog" asking the "overdog" a question and having the "overdog" respond. Continue this and see what happens. Normally the "underdog" will come up to a par with the "overdog" and a good gestalt will have happened within your own soul. This dialogue can also take place with two chairs facing each other where you start sitting in one chair as either the "underdog" or "overdog" and move back and forth as you continue to dialogue. You may also wish to have a gestalt dialogue between any person or object in the dream and yourself.

10. Put a title at the top of the dream.

11. What action does the dream call for, if any? It may be calling for a concrete action: take a serious look at my vocation or slow down. The action called for may be symbolic, such as putting a symbol from your dream on your refrigerator or painting a picture of the dream or being aware of birds which remind you of the dream.

12. Is there any humor in your dream? There is a lot of humor that occurs in dreams. Sometimes we need to just laugh at the humor. At other times, the humor holds deep meaning for us. If, in our dream, there is an elephant in our living room, it causes us to laugh. But then the serious message begins to dawn on us. The dream maker is especially trying to draw our attention to that part of the dream. See what meaning the humor has for you.

13. The dream may also call for extensive research on anything that occurs in your dream that you know little or nothing about.

Appendix B

THE HADEN INSTITUTE GUIDELINES
FOR DREAM GROUPS

All participants should have had some previous exposure to dreams whether it is extensive reading or a period of recording their own dreams or an introductory course or conference or individual meetings with someone on dreams.

No one should be coerced to come to the group. Everyone should feel good and comfortable and safe being there. If your psyche is telling you now is not the time, wait. If you are seeing a therapist, consult with him or her about being in the group.

It is best to have someone in leadership of the group who is versed in dream work and group process. If not, use a rotating convener who sees that the group sticks to its rules for its own safety.

Every gathering of the group should begin with silence, the ringing of a bell, lighting of a candle, Jesus prayer or some ritual that will center the group and invoke God's spirit. Every gathering should end with participants in a circle holding hands sharing an extemporaneous prayer time or the Lord's Prayer or something that will gather all you have done together in that session. This closing ritual is a reminder of God's grace, a reminder that all are accepted regardless of where they are on their journey.

The group can then spend 20 minutes or so checking in with each other. It is important to share something of your life and any relevant information or feelings. This will help the trust and encourage connections between your life and your dreams.

Then the leader or someone previously appointed gives a fifteen-minute presentation on the wisdom of the dream or related material. This presentation can come from ancient or modern sources. It can make use of Jungian psychology or mythology or scripture or a book or tape on the subject matter. A short period of reaction or discussion can follow. This practice, along with the opening prayer, calls forth the Self, not only bringing in wisdom, but also promoting health, healing and safety within the group.

Everyone who wishes now shares a dream. No discussion or interpretation, just the actual dream. If there is not enough time, they can share a title for their dream.

The leader can now ask for a volunteer to share his or her dream for group work. Preference should be given to anyone who has not presented a dream before. The procedure, at this point, should be strictly as follows:

1. The person shares the dream, just the dream (not their interpretation).
2. The group asks questions of clarification (not interpretation).
3. The leader now asks the dream presenter to give the dream to the group and to turn her or his chair away from the group. Doing so helps the group feel as if the dream is truly theirs. This practice also keeps the dreamer from the need to respond.
4. The group will now talk with each other as the dreamer listens. The group now projects onto the dream using the words "if it were my dream…" or "in my dream…." It is important to the process that the group adheres to these two rules.
5. After sufficient exploration of the dream, invite the dreamer back into the group. Thank him or her for sharing and tell her or him that it is important to track their dreams in the next few days, because future dreams will repeat what the dreamer did not catch. Thus, we do not have to worry about milking every "aha" out of every dream. Dreamwork is a continuing process.
6. Remind the group members that they were projecting onto the dream. So, have them recall what they said and ask if they make any connections with the energies and issues inside them. Even if no one speaks up, the question has been established and they will be making connections during the day. This process also takes the spotlight off the dreamer and puts it back on the group.

Conclude with a closing prayer circle.

Appendix C

THE HADEN INSTITUTE
DREAM GROUP AND DREAM
TRAINING ETHICAL GUIDELINES

The Haden Institute adopts the ethics statements of the International
Association for the Study of Dreams [see below] and adds the following:

- Every dream group should be in the container of the spiritual for its safety
  and wisdom. Dreams put us in touch with the Divine as well as personal and
  social growth and problem solving.

- Although much good therapy happens as a by-product of dream groups and
  The Haden Institute Dream Leader Training, dream work is not meant to be
  psychotherapy. We encourage good therapy with a professional when desired.

- All dream groups, regardless of the method used, should preface comments on
  another's dreams with "if it were my dream" or "in my dream." This is a way
  to minimize, own, and acknowledge projection.

IASD DREAMWORK ETHICS STATEMENT

IASD celebrates the many benefits of dreamwork, yet recognizes that there are
potential risks. IASD supports an approach to dreamwork and dream sharing
that respects the dreamer's dignity and integrity; and which recognizes the
dreamer as the decision-maker regarding the significance of the dream. Systems
of dreamwork that assign authority over, or knowledge of the dream's meanings
to someone who is not the dreamer can be misleading, incorrect and harmful.
Ethical dreamwork helps the dreamer work with his or her own dream images,
feelings, associations, etc., and guides the dreamer to more fully experience,
appreciate and understand the dream. Every dream may have multiple
meanings, and different techniques may be reasonably employed to touch these
multiple layers of significance.

A dreamer's decision to share or discontinue sharing a dream should always be
respected and honored. The dreamer should be forewarned that unexpected
issues or emotions may arise in the course of dreamwork. Information and
mutual agreement about the degree of privacy and confidentiality are essential
ingredients in creating a safe atmosphere for dream sharing.

Dreamwork outside of a clinical setting is not a substitute for psychotherapy, or other professional treatment, and should not be used as such.

IASD recognizes and respects that there are many valid and time-honored dreamwork traditions. We invite and welcome participation of dreamers from all cultures. There are social, cultural and transpersonal aspects to dream experience. In this statement we do not mean to imply that the only valid approach to dreamwork focuses on the dreamer's personal life. Our purpose is to honor and respect the person of the dreamer as well as the dream itself, regardless of how the relationship between the two may be understood.

Appendix D

DREAM BIBLIOGRAPHY
RECOMMENDED BY THE HADEN INSTITUTE

Achroyd, Eric - *A Dictionary of Dream Symbols*

Bosnak, Robert – *A Little Course in Dreams*

Brook, Stephen – *The Oxford Book of Dreams*

Bryant, Dorothy – *The Kin of Atta Are Waiting for You*

Campbell, Joseph, ed. – *Myths, Dreams and Religion*

Cirlot, J.E. – *A Dictionary of Symbols*

Clift, Jean and Wallace – *Symbols of Transformation in Dreams*

Fontana, David – *The Secret Language of Dreams*

Freud, Sigmund – *The Interpretation of Dreams*

Gongloff, Robert – *Dream Exploration*

* Haden, Robert – *Unopened Letters from God*

Hall, James – *Jungian Dream Interpretation*

Hoss, Robert – *Dream Language*

* Hudson, Joyce Rockwood – *Natural Spirituality*

Johnson, Robert A. – *Inner Work*

Jung, Carl Gutav – *Dreams*

Jung, Carl Gutav – *Man and His Symbols*

* Jung, Carl Gutav – *Memories, Dreams and Reflections*

Jung, Carl Gutav – *Psychology and Religion*

Kelsey, Morton – *Dreams: A Way to Listen to God*

Kelsey, Morton – *God, Dreams and Revelation*

Kutz, Ilan – *Dreamland Comparison*

Lyons, Tallula – *Dream Prayers*

Maurer, Sue – *God Has Been Whispering in My Ear*

Moore, Thomas – *The Care of the Soul*

Moore, Thomas – *Soul Mates*

* Sanford, John – *Dreams: God's Forgotten Language*

Sanford, John – *Dreams and Healing*

Sanford, John – *Healing and Wholeness*

Sanford, John – *Invisible Partners*

Sanford, John – *The Kingdom Within*

Sanford, John – *The Man Who Wrestled With God*

Savary, Louise – *Dreams & Spiritual Growth*

Singer, June – *Boundaries of the Soul*

Stein, Murray, ed. – *Jungian Analysis*

Stevens, Anthony – *Achetypes*

*   Taylor, Jeremy – *The Wisdom of Your Dream*

Taylor, Jeremy – *Dream Work*

Van de Castle, Robert L. – *Our Dreaming Mind*

von Franz, Marie-Louise – *Animus and Anima*

von Franz, Marie-Louise – *On Dreams and Death*

von Franz, Marie-Louise – *Projection and Re-Collection*

Welch, John – *Spiritual Pilgrims: Carl Jung and Teresa of Avila*

* Good Beginning Books

Appendix E

JUNGIAN TERMINOLOGY

The most concise and accessible definition of **Jungian psychology** is that it is the dialogue between the conscious and the unconscious.

The **conscious** is everything we are aware of in waking life. Jung's **personal unconscious** is what Freud meant by the subconscious. It contains things we once knew, but have repressed. For Freud that was the totality of the unconscious. Jung expanded the understanding of the unconscious to the **collective unconscious** and pointed to evidence for its existence. The **collective unconscious** is the universal storehouse of symbols and history that everyone shares.

The **ego** and the **persona** are found in the **conscious** aspect of the individual. **Shadows** and **Anima/Animus** are found in the personal unconscious. The Anima/Animus acts as a bridge to the collective unconscious. **Complexes** are in the personal unconscious but with an archetypical center connecting it to the collective unconscious. **Archetypes** are found in the collective unconscious.

Amplification: The elaboration and clarification of a dream-image by making personal associations and parallel associations from such things as myth, scripture, symbol, folklore, and religion. The process of amplification with aspects of your dream can lead to deeper insight, meaningful connections and important discoveries that produce instant healings and insights.

Anima: The unconscious feminine side of a man's nature. The Anima is usually personified in dreams by persons of the opposite sex. The Anima also acts as a bridge from the psyche to the collective unconscious.

Animus: The unconscious masculine side of a woman's nature. The animus is usually personified in dreams by persons of the opposite sex. The Animus also acts as a bridge from the psyche to the collective unconscious.

Archetype: Universal patterns or motifs that come from the collective unconscious and are the basic content of religions, mythologies, legends and fairy tales. Archetypes emerge in individuals in the form of dreams, visions and fantasies. Example: The wise old man or the wise old woman who appears in dreams, literature and film.

Complex: Feeling-toned energies that over the years accumulate around certain archetypes. You can be well aware that you have touched someone's complex when they respond with a 'hell no' or some similar feeling-packed words and/or body movement. Complexes are autonomous. They are like separate personalities. Reason has little impact on complexes. Dreams provide direct access to the complexes. A way to get at complexes is to ask "where in your life have you experienced feelings like those released in a particular dream?" Jung's association test is a good way to surface complexes. Jung said, "We don't have complexes; complexes have us until we become conscious of them." Complexes are both positive and negative. Complexes are necessary to life. Complexes are shaped and influenced by archetypes, culture and family history and relationships. We are familiar with inferiority complexes, mother or father complexes, Napoleonic complexes, but there are hundreds of complexes. An excessively strong reaction and the stories in our dreams are two primary ways to bring a complex to consciousness.

Constellate: To stir psychic contents in the unconscious in such a way that its effects are perceived and felt in your conscious world. For example, just going to see a physician, spiritual director, priest or therapist can constellate the healer archetype.

Ego: The center of consciousness; what we think of when we say "I."

Individuation: Growth towards wholeness and that into which God is calling us. It is a life-long process with dark nights as well as mountain-top experiences.

Numinous: Experiences of The Holy that seem to come from exterior sources. Jung said, "The approach to the numinous is the real therapy and inasmuch as you attain to the numinous experiences you are released from the curse of pathology."

Persona: (Latin for actor's mask) One's social role, derived from society's expectations and early training. A strong ego has a flexible persona. Jung explained that personas are helpful. We get in trouble when we identify with one persona like doctor, lawyer, teacher, preacher or mother, father, wife, husband. It is helpful and healthy to move into all of our personas at the appropriate time; for example switching from our blue jean persona, to our clergy persona, to our mama persona, to our fun persona, etc.

Psyche: All of the human being which is not physical; the dynamic process, conscious and unconscious, which makes up the human personality.

Self: The archetype of wholeness and the regulating center of the psyche; a transpersonal power that transcends the ego. Some speak of this as the God-within or the Christ-within. The Self is the author of dreams. The Self is always promoting healing and wholeness, even through nightmares and dark nights.

Shadow: An unconscious part of the personality characterized by traits and attitudes, whether negative or positive, that a person refuses to accept or ignores, often at his or her own peril. There are BRIGHT shadows as well as DARK shadows. Identifying your heroes and heroines and the figures you admire in your dreams will give you clues to your dormant bright shadow. Excessive emotion on your part in waking life and dark figures as well as persons of the same sex in your dreams can help you identify your dark shadow. Our Shadow is unconscious to us. To the extent that our shadow remains unconscious, it is automatically projected onto society. And the energy of that projection caught unconsciously by others causes them to be darker (or brighter) than they are. Our healing work is the re-collection of our projections. Our first task is to recognize it. Jung said the good thing about projection is that we have to see it in projected form before we can identify it in ourselves. The second task is to make friends with our shadow. One of the best ways to do this is circumambulating our dreams, especially the unlikable characters and the people of the same sex. We do not have to totally act out our shadows, but we are asked to make friends with them. The continuing task is to romance the shadow in a multitude of ways.

Synchronicity: A meaningful coincidence. A synchronistic event occurs when an inward event (dream, vision, premonition) is seen to have a connection in external reality. Example: A person has a dream about meeting a close friend he or she hasn't seen in years and the next day runs into that friend. Another example would be the Chinese saying, "when the student is ready, the teacher appears." Synchronicities cannot be explained in any rational way. Jean Shinoda Bolen says that "At the most profound level, synchronicities can lead us to the awareness that we are a part of something far greater than ourselves, and to a sense of wholeness in the archetype of the Self, metaphorically expressed by the Grail Legend, by the concept of the Kingdom of God, or by returning to the Tao."

Transcendent Function: The reconciling new perspective that arises from the unconscious when we hold the opposites in tension. Jung encourages us to hold the tension long enough to know what the deeper soul issues are. The transcendent function is sometimes referred to as the transcendent third.

Transference-Counter Transference: A particular kind of projection spoken of in the spiritual director, priest, doctor, or therapeutic relationship. Transference is the unconscious projection from the client to the therapist. Counter-transference is the unconscious projection of the therapist onto the client. One of the positive aspects of this is that the client normally projects the healer archetype onto the therapist which constellates healing into the session. The therapist keeps his or her counter-transference at a healthy level by doing her or his own spiritual and psychological work.

Appendix F

DREAM WORKSHOP DVD SERIES

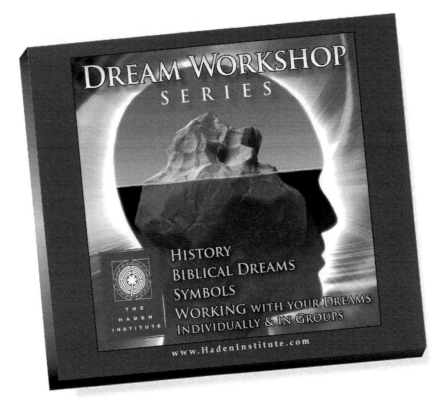

This DVD series is for use with:
- Dream Group Leaders beginning a new Dream Group
- Conferences, Workshops & Weekend Retreats
- Spiritual Directors, Clergy, Counselors
- Adult Classes & Seminars
- Weekday or Evening Series
- Those wanting to know how to work with their own dreams
- Those who want to know more about the dream world, especially as it relates to spirituality and personal growth

Available at: www.hadeninstitute.com or call 828-693-9292
Cost: $49 per DVD set (Plus Shipping & Handling)

Appendix G

A tradition was begun in the summer of 2003 – a major conference for all who want to recover the ancient Biblical tradition of listening for God's word in our nightly dreams.

We have had a large crowd with increasing numbers every summer.

- Designed for new and returning participants
- Keynote lectures
- Dream groups
- 24 practical workshops
- Outdoor and indoor worship, music, the Kanuga Labyrinth, and all the gifts of the Blue Ridge Mountains in early summer.

The conference is held every year at Kanuga Conference Center, Hendersonville, NC.

For more information and to register: www.hadeninstitute.com

Appendix H

TWO YEAR COURSE IN DREAM LEADER TRAINING

This two-year course is for Therapists, Clergy and Individuals who wish to lead dream groups or enhance their therapeutic skills.

The purpose of this training program is four-fold:
- To train and certify people to lead church and community dream groups
- To help professionals and others to integrate dreamwork into their chosen vocation
- To enhance and encourage responsible dreamwork across the nation
- To help recover the ancient Biblical tradition of listening for God's word for us in our nightly dreams

The Program is designed for:
Therapists who wish to enhance their therapeutic skills; parishioners, lay leaders, and clergy who wish to lead church dream groups; community group leaders who wish to learn dream group skills; and those who wish to go deeper into the dream world.

The major portion of each Intensive is spent in teaching/dialogue with faculty and Dream Practicum Groups with faculty support. There are also socials, videos, dramas, demonstrations, sharing, Dream Theatre, relaxation and fun in the Blue Ridge Mountains of North Carolina.

The Program Includes:
- The History of Dreams
- Dream Symbolism
- Individual Dream Work
- Group Dream Work
- The Use of Dreams in Therapy, Spiritual Guidance, and Vocational Discernment
- The Basics of Jungian Psychology
- Dream Research
- Majoring in an Aspect of the Dream where Participant's Energy is High
- Reading and Reports in the Broad Field of Dreams
- Individuation Work with a Dream Counselor
- Training as a Dream Group Leader

Teaching and Certification
Methods of teaching include: Didactic, Experiential, Case Study, Dialogical and Meditative. A certificate will be awarded upon successful completion. CEUs are available (NBCC and NASW).

Appendix I

TWO YEAR COURSE IN
SPIRITUAL DIRECTION TRAINING

This training is available in the US and Canada. The US training is held at Kanuga Conference Center, Hendersonville, NC. It consists of three four-day weekends per year plus distance learning. The Canadian program is held at Mt. Carmel Spiritual Centre, Niagara Falls, Canada. It meets two separate weeks (fall and spring) per year plus distance learning.

The purpose of this training program is four-fold:
- To train and certify people to be Spiritual Directors in the Jungian, Mystical, Dream, and Christian Tradition
- To help professionals and others integrate the spiritual dimension into their chosen vocation
- To honor lay and ordained Spiritual Directors
- To offer Spiritual Direction Training that is open to the wisdom of all faith traditions, east and west

The Program is designed for:
- Therapists who want to integrate a spiritual dimension to their counseling
- Ministers who want to deepen this aspect of their ministry
- Twelve Step Workers who want to increase their spiritual skills and wisdom
- Judges and Lawyers seeking spiritual dimension in their decisions and life
- Nurses, physicians, hospice workers, and medical personnel looking for a closer connection to the spiritual dimension of healing
- Business and Political leaders who want to be more grounded as servant leaders
- Persons who wish to have a primary vocation or avocation as a Spiritual Director
- Individuals who want to take their spiritual lives more seriously

Ancient Forms of Spirituality Relevant to Our Day
The Dream, the Labyrinth, the Jesus Breath Prayer, Desert Spirituality, Celtic Spirituality, Enneagrams, Typology, Centering Prayer, Guided Meditation, Journal Writing, Mythology, Poetry, Silence and Ritual, and Dante's Divine Comedy.

Grounding In

Spiritual Discernment, Jungian Psychology, The Feminine Face of God, Group Spirituality, Care of the Soul, Mind/Body, Other Religions, and the best in DVDs and CDs.

Small Group Experiences
- Spiritual Autobiographies
- Group Spirituality
- Lectio Divina
- Spiritual Direction Case Studies
- Dream Group
- Labyrinth Walk
- Poetry Writing

Teaching and Certification

Methods of teaching include: Didactic, Experiential, Case Study, Dialogical and Meditative. A certificate will be awarded upon successful completion. CEUs are available (NBCC and NASW).

For more information and to register see www.hadeninstitute.com or call 828-693-9292.

FOR MORE RESOURCES AND INFORMATION VISIT

www.HadenInstitute.com

Purchase the book online at:
www.hadeninstitute.com

39602118R00120

Made in the USA
Lexington, KY
02 March 2015